UPGRADED MENTAL SOFTWARE INSIDE

- Improved Ram
- Improved bus speed
- All Card Reader ports included
- Unlimited High Bandwidth

  following upgrade
- Wireless at Giga Byte speed
- Always connected
- Never needs reboot
- Terabyte Hard Disk

Benefits begin immediately once upgrade is completed.

ALSO BY B.J. DOHRMANN

Money Magic

♦

Super Achievers

♦

Diamond Heart

♦

Redemption

♦

Perfection "CAN" Be Had

Published by Life Success Academy

200 Lime Quarry Road

Madison, Alabama 35758

(256) 774-5444

SUPER ACHIEVER
MINDSETS

BY BJ DOHRMANN

To my two young boys, Ryan and Justin.

The day you changed your legal names to Dohrmann was the
day you adopted "me." I'll never have a better day,
my two Super Achievers.

TABLE OF CONTENTS

SNAP

Super Networking Accelerates Potential (SNAP) is an acronym for the federally trademarked process of faster networking known in corporate circles as SNAP. SNAP is an exercise for the most important muscle the body possesses, the muscle of the Mind. Perhaps, it is the first new exercise for the muscle of the Mind in 100 years. SNAP assists men and women from all walks of life to live their futures as SUPER ACHIEVING human beings......

<u>NOTE</u>: In November of 1992 George Bush, Sr. joined four other men in the past century to be turned away by the American voters in favor of a new direction. This rejection largely took place due to the issues of the domestic economy vs. the international peace. Historically, it is clear that Bill Clinton out-SNAPed George Bush. At an earlier, happier time for the Bushes, I was taught a lesson by George on the subject of Networking - the skill of the century. As my book is about SUPER ACHIEVER success, and success itself depends on mastering networking, I have opened my story with George Bush, Sr., one of my own great teachers. I believe his son, a much later President of the United States, has mastered the lesson his Dad taught me in the 1980's. I hope you profit from the story.

GEORGE BUSH IS A SNAPPER TOO

I can remember thinking as I left in my new tuxedo for the $2,500-a-plate Republican dinner at the famous St. Francis Hotel ballroom, "My life IS a bit of a real life movie." In fact, I have had others **plus** this idea by reminding me...... "You know B.J.; a lot of people pay money, then wait in line, buy popcorn, find a seat, settle down and really enjoy the excitement of watching a movie, a movie that <u>you</u> live in real life every day." Of course, when you're living your life you don't **think** your own life is all that interesting. You're too busy living it. When I stop and think about it, there is probably more than one book, one movie, in everyone's life. <u>People are more interesting than fiction.</u>

That night in San Francisco was like a movie set. I had given up the opportunity, which Gary Shansby (then head of the three-hundred-million-dollar Shaklee Corporation) had offered the night before, the privilege to sit at the head table beside George and Barbara Bush in the lush ballroom of the St. Francis Hotel. Like many people I find it embarrassing to support something you believe in and then sit and look at all those people while they stare back at you. I opted to sit in the sea of round tables, ornately established for Bay Area leading business executives. I chose to sit with insurance executive Don Schlesser, who drove across the "other Bridge" from Danville just to meet George and

Barbara. There might have been others with colorful pasts in the room that night besides me – but I personally felt "how weird" the Secret Service treated me like royalty that night. Or was it over and had I been redeemed somewhere along the way?

I was after all joining all the king's men and sitting at the king's table.

Upon arrival the VIP guests were treated to dog inspection. Jump-suited special force teams were combing the hotel isles on every floor, both below and above where George would soon hold court. We, the dignitaries, were carefully screened by molded people in blue coats who came from their rubber stamp factories complete with tiny little pins. I marveled how they talked into their lapels, sometimes with a preference to speak instead into their coat sleeves. It made almost normal people smile more than once. Years before Terror became a hot topic; these "ladies in waiting" were practicing to get it all right the very first time. We were impressed.

Some took longer to clear "Checkpoint Charlie" than others. It put a chill on a social climber now and again, given their VIP status. Not to mention all the money San Francisco had contributed in a single night by the Bay.

Annoyance (frosted by a tinge of arrogance) ran high from some of the larger donors. Being one of those larger contributors to the night's festivities, I was finding it all a great amusement. Everyone was tipping high to be seen, as well as to SEE, over the line up ahead - an indiscreet type of tip-toe that the wealthy perform as a ballet, much like stretching innocuously. The cream was showing up....the bankers, the stock brokers, the business owners, the captains of trade with Japan....the elite....courting favor, glad-handing the new important connection. Power is a funny thing. For those in the know, power really is only a decision. Make the right decision and you possess power. Make the wrong decision and you dine watching the play from the streets. All too many let others make their most crucial life decisions for them resulting in power-LESS lifestyles.

Make the wrong decision (or no decision at all) and power is a vapor dissipating in the rolling eddies of life. I study power and tonight was my classroom. I was finding the feeling of power like standing near a Hoover Dam turbine as the flow gates opened and the concrete and steel beneath your feet began to shake. I was in a great downtown hotel, but I could feel the San Francisco ground shaking with the power, and I was thinking, "This isn't an earthquake B.J. – it's just raw old Global Power having a dinner party."

Smiling behind my coveted gold embossed VIP arrival envelope, I gave "Mr. NO NAME" my welcome package. After speaking into his left coat sleeve, I was one of the lucky ones, for in only moments the good news arrived from the Starship Enterprise that I would now be permitted to amble on over to the elevator. I turned the marble embossed corner only to discover the elevator was held hostage by more blue coats in waiting. Knowing I was not a sex symbol but nevertheless enjoying all the attention, I swirled into the elevator with the crowd of fashion, furs and diamonds.

My blue eyes observed the mahogany-stained elevator doors looked like giant library book ends as they parted to let us exit from this upward mobility. The wide carpeted hallways were embroidered with threads of gold, from interlaced patterns, to pentagons to ceilings imported from France, the opulence was noted. The entourage, Sneezy, Dopey and Doc reminded me more of the Queen's deck of "CARD GUARDS" in the magic rose garden from *Alice in Wonderland*. Sleepy and Grumpy were nearby, spaced like pillars of steel, as the blue brigade formed the gauntlet first on one side, then on the other, making a cordial but clear security path for the guests, and later for President Bush himself. The "ushers" directed the elegant people into the deeply entrenched cocktail party. Twenty foot high Victorian windows brought San Francisco Bay into clear perspective. The Golden Gate Bridge and Alcatraz Island marked the twilight bringing sanity to the affairs of state – a fact not lost on this fifth generation legacy child to the city.

Drink in hand, every guest had the nervous air that is imparted when royalty approaches, the ceremony uniquely American, the traditions exciting and uncommon. Small talk dotted the air sounding like the patter of rain. No one was serious quite yet, after all court was not officially "in session."

After far too long a political wait (and no small speculation the unforeseen had once again put off the appearance of power) the announcement was made: "Would the guests kindly join George Bush in the anti room." The surprise location made yet another parade as the rich and famous pretended to walk imaginary dogs, each taking their time, when all they wanted to do was RUN and throw themselves prostrate to kiss the papal ring. As our party (I remember they called it "our party" for some reason) made its way down one new aisle, it seemed the entire parade of Blue Coats, trench coats, jumpsuits and police dogs had been lined up for our personal inspection, one last time. I saluted more than one, sometimes with no more than a wink. Not even a wince of a smile in return flowed my way. Our U.S. finest, like Buckingham Palace's dressed Reds at their best, lack a common sense of humor. I always admire Britain's unsmiling castle guards' stony countenance, but they hold nothing over the American Secret Service.

Suddenly, there "he" was. Carrying the White House on his pinky ring and matching the word POWER with demeanor and a lapel button that said the Eagle HAS landed. One had to pause and reflect with a furrow to the forehead, that certain men (and women) exhale power like a breath, and carry the honor well, regardless of whether you agree on the politics or not. The sheer majesty of it all was lost on no one, regardless of party.

I moved away from the seat of authority and the line in front of it, without addressing the need for a greeting, to a more comfortable position by the bar, somewhat remote to those seeking a POWER POSITION near the throne. Watching the **great ones** grovel for a handshake and titter for a moment as the fund-raiser brings its reward....the ritual of money....the engine of state in its highest gear....White House cruise control locked down and holding. I was soaking in sights and speculation, making eye contact only now and again as I observed from my perch....

A diamond necklace Tiffany's would safeguard in a time-locked safe....a sable from Russia....just a few peacocks out for a hoot at the St. Francis...a designer gown priced to upstage the impetuous...and who would even THINK to ask......

I could not help but reflect on the history of this gold rush/earthquake survivor, this St. Francis....Emerald to San Francisco....host to Union Squares from around the world. The Queen of England joins Presidents from Hoover to Bush...the Royals, the Prime Ministers, the authors, the movie stars. And not the least of which was the passing thought that my grandfather, Albert Bernhard Charles Dohrmann for whom I was named, was a founding partner who rebuilt this Hotel following its destruction in 1906. I was thinking as I looked over the city that the castle was built by my grandfather, as part of his West Coast Family empire, and I raised a glass to the Golden Gate and my namesake. Such is the fifth-generation heritage of a native San Franciscan, a lot for an Alabama transplant to consider.

There was a quiet nod when George Bush caught my eye on more than one occasion. Then came the "come on over" gesture which the popcorn crunchers sitting in their swayback movie chairs would not fail to catch. It was more the "I-know-you-but-I-can't-remember-who-you-are look" suggesting I may be someone important. After all, there were only two or three of us that had not lined up to say hello and HE knew who each of us was and where in the room that night we resided. He was now paying special attention to "us" and it was quite well noticed to the envy of the early birds.

For in the game of SNAPing – many are called but few are chosen.

Eventually, when out of respect for too many handshakes and too much crushing intimacy, body space opened around the President's drink hand, I suggested a handshake and reintroduced myself. The "Oh yes, I remember" when I was sure he didn't was the feeling, but still it was charming as he and Barbara always made themselves so gracious in every setting.

The conventional, "So, what are you doing these days?" began, though the keen eyes sharpened a bit as the former CIA director reflected on my response.

"Well, George, I leave for Israel tomorrow. Moshe Dyan is not well these days, and I want to spend some time with him and Rachel." In fact, mine would be one of the last hands he graced, and the dedicated last book he wrote still resides from that trip in my bookshelf to this very day.

In the moment following the required small talk about my importing business in Ancient Art from the Holy Land (I was one of the larger antiquity dealers in the world at the time), the talk turned into a direction that surprised even me.

"You know, B.J. ," George was taking a good deal of time with me while other guests seem to follow White House body language that conveyed - Buzz-off for a moment - "We just put our AWAC resources and other high technology tools in the hands of the Saudi Arabian government. (I liked the nasal twang of his voice as he rotated by the window to avoid the proximity of another gaze or foiled handshake). I don't have to tell you, (you) doing business over in that part of the world, how important these systems are." He had a quite way of talking; bending over slightly from his body tower, so that no one else heard the offerings.

I was shifting on my feet as the conversation was going into some areas that I was reading about in the news. I had only just read that we were CONSIDERING giving the Saudi people high technology defense systems. I had not read that we HAD given them possession of such critical resources yet, but then, I was having a cocktail with the White House in San Francisco. I trusted the source of information.

"I'd be real interested in what Moshe Dyan would have to say about our position on all this, B.J. Off the record....Unofficial. He might ask some of their leaders and give us some off channel feedback. Let him KNOW it's all off the record. We just want to have an easy read. You up for that?"

"In fact, we wouldn't mind knowing just how he saw the Knesset (Israelis Congress) and the various leadership factions are going to privately beyond the public stand, actually settle in for our position here. I'd like to know how THEY see the direction our new policies are taking us and any comments THEY might want to share from this back channel." He offered a big flashy smile as he completed his "SNAP" request.

After some thought I asked, "So, Mr. President, how do I let you know about the dinner conversations I may enjoy next week?"

He patted my hand as he said, "Call me George" then, he winked and said, "just write me a personal letter." He said it with a twang and a big grin. "You know where I live. THEY'LL get it to me"...and I presupposed "they" would too.

I remember (coming out of the trance of it) that time seemed to have gone still during those unexpected minutes of small talk. SNAP Requests (where power exists) are like that. Snappers recognize opportunities, and they are quick to SNAP such opportunities up. I don't know how long we actually talked about the important stuff, say ten minutes. I was told, it was longer than anyone else talked to the leader of the free world that night. I do remember that it must have been awhile. It seemed like a year for some reason.

The small talk was small talk. Took only seconds.

The other stuff seemed to stall actual **time** into some strange kind of loop. I remember thinking a lot about that the rest of the evening. In fact, George was called away on an emergency aboard Air Force One that night (added a bit of drama when Barbara and he left that way) as they had to cut the much-anticipated dinner speech short. Upon reflection, this made our time and chat the high point of the night. More than one of San Francisco's elite came to ask that night, "What was THAT all about?"

All of it made you feel like the entire purpose of attending the event was the time warp of our private chat, as if Destiny was inside. True or not, it felt sweeter than fine wine, as power transfers always will.

As a teacher, on the subject of power, I would consider much later that George and I were keenly AWARE of what we were saying to each other. We held a calm knowing of the routine of events at the top. There are men who study and apply lessons of power (not to make the session overly important) as only one more stream of catching opportunities that fine leadership represents when perfectly practiced.

I reflected, over the red sauce and service, pensively to myself, "How many people tonight discussed what even the newspapers have yet to report? How many people have even a small sidebar mission to play for the benefit of the White House, the

Gulf and the world?" I knew my friend Rafi Brown and Professor Amnon Bentor would be pleased, as well they should, when they would drive me to General Dyan's home. I became the mock turtle and picked up my glass and toasted to the empty chair George had, only recently, vacated and said so quietly to my own self-talk ..... "Life is Good, President George, Life is Good!" I toasted a true master in Super Networking, the warp drive motor of power for the developing Global Village. SNAP it to 'em, Mr. President. Then, I drank the wine, of course.

LEARNING FROM LIFE

I commuted to Israel...the twenty-seven-hour "long way" from San Francisco via Athens. Service held less terror and better food in those long-gone "once upon a time" days. I hated Athens from my first trip in, to recent history. In oceans of obsolescence, dirt and grime, amid a sea of anti-Christian intolerance, one feels a sense of being unsafe, as an American passing the time in a throng of men and women darkly-attired as their local custom requires. Most of the long journey's time was invested in lap computers and international corporate work. Long forgotten efforts I was reasonably certain some unknown Mossad Israeli would one day copy as I clicked to transmit to our mainframe computers after my arrival at the King David Hotel. In an information age, being the first kid on your block to master everything new is an imperative, not a luxury, in business – no one traveling had a lap top in those days – and I felt like such a big dog. I think, if memory serves me well, I had the CPU power of today's wrist watch, or perhaps a bit less.

I spent some quality time after a shower, shave and sunset over the Old Walls of Jerusalem, with my once dear friends Moshe Dyan and Rachel. I believe the tiny cup of "coffee" (pre-Starbucks) – practically ate my spoon, if I recall it correctly. The phrase "one cup will do ya" comes to mind. Another dear friend, Rafi Brown, the famous archeologist who originally opened and ultimately displayed the Dead Sea scrolls at the Shrine of the Book in Tel Aviv (former head of Authentication for Antiquities at Israel Museum) had joined our dinner party. Live comedy, Rafi had us laughing until the early dawn. Sometime during the night, I can't pinpoint when this late in the game, we discussed my recent meeting with George Bush and his casual request at the St. Francis Hotel in San Francisco related to AWACS and military technology of the time.

My wife and I were used to dealing with many Gulf-based Arab friendships creating a political bridge making of our core Ancient Art business – trading between Arab interest and Jewish interest in an art that had become second nature. Every business deal was a treaty. The conversation held ripples of implications on the surface and deep below where the submarines prowl.

On the long flight home, I wrote my report and sent it off to the White House and thought no more about the exercise in CEO-to-CEO networking. In fact, I was more preoccupied with the sadness of Moshe Dyan's cancer, as the Israeli General was about to meet his personal graduation - and I would miss his genius, history and reflections, but never his coffee. This tough, one-eyed general from Israel was not a warrior to my family; he was a personal friend and mentor. His last letter to me hangs on the wall in my office.

Later, much later, I put the event in some new perspective. I knew that Alvin Toffler, author of *Future Shock*, and best-selling trend forecasters like Mark Victor Hansen's *One Minute Millionaire* and others focused on the key skill of networking as breath to the success mechanism. NETWORKING, it seemed, was the core master skill to seek out in the new century for CEOs who wished to prosper and more importantly to LEAD.

NETWORKING was the master passkey for success in leadership at the top – a boardroom barometer.

As I began to teach courses on NETWORKING and later SUPER NETWORKING (our invention for Fortune Companies see www.ibiglobal.com) to CEOs - I appreciated how leadership instinctively recognizes instant opportunity. .

George Bush seized every chance to benefit from SUPER NETWORKING as naturally as breathing air in the Rose Garden. Super Networking – a CEO skill to instantly use every contact and key connection to obtain new information, **perhaps valuable** information, useful to the nation NOW versus "never" - is a leadership instinct at CEO leadership level of play. To put information to its highest and best use, an application of making more and better DECISIONS is a highly practiced art form for every corporate leader.

CEO TIP: Study and train on the topic of applied SUPER NETWORKING from the best corporate retreat trainers whenever they are offered on this subject. Your new "team" skills in Super Networking will create core improvements in your near term performance – which is why you bring the inside team to make the outside dream work faster.

By networking, George Bush helped to topple the Berlin Wall, ended the cold war, ended Soviet Union Communism with FREEDOMISM and opened democracies in more than a dozen nations all over the world. In fact, all this time later, the Bush family is still spreading democracy and freedom around the world like a healthy epidemic. From Afghanistan to Iraq, peace is breaking out under a Bush Super Team Networking Span that is reforming the global village in a single generation. By networking, George W. Bush, during the recession of 2002 & 2003, kept the world banking system together and brought home recession-killer planning that is even today helping the entire world step into full partnership with prosperity.

Post Terror history was established by the SUPER NETWORK-

ING strength George had exhibited before I instructed my first Super Networking course – by a team who wrote the ground rules by "doing" them. In recent history, his son's vision is engineering an alliance that unites a world against atomic rogue nations and terror wherever it appears, using super networks of technology – one of which we call STAR WARS.

NETWORKING IS THE SKILL OF THE CENTURY....
AND EVERYONE KNOWS IT!

Networking leadership, both in politics and free enterprise, delivers the goods....better decisions and improved performance, whenever leaders retrain themselves to apply master networking advanced technology against day-to-day resolution execution.

A growing, international, experienced team of educators has been gaining data that Super Networking is a key master skill which defines the new Global Village as a market place. Those who master the Global Village marketable skill of Super Networking become defector LEADERS inside this rapidly developing planetary market place. Super Teaching is a master skill acquired one mind at a time....a **process** that both leads and defines the excitement of our shrinking global village economy. SNAP (Super Networking Accelerates Potential) leaders are recognized by their teams for making better and more frequent decisions, all of the time, every hour....every second....every moment they have to command authority. As competition is replaced with cooperation as a vital systemic corporate decision, networking and SUPER NETWORKING draw upon electronic, now wireless, and soon global wireless, planetary markets to open vast seas of connections far beyond the performance potential of the old competition model.

Mastering faster, smarter use of new networking resources shapes leaders rather than the other way around. Super Networking is a warp drive relationship builder. Old forms represent covered-wagon relationship building tools that have become obsolete with the Star Fleet of Global economies.

This key concept is helping leaders in education to SNAP globally as they better educate by practicing the network models they teach to tomorrow's global village leaders. Leaders are either shapers of the new economy or they become victims of the new economy. Leaders who shape this brave new world transform their communities, states and nations. In fact, they help all of us, as global Directors, who contribute to usher in the new world peace. The bi-product of cooperation systems vs. competition systems in the work environment is world peace.

No sustainable economic progress can be realized from the current competitive model. Competitive problem solving has taken mankind as far as it can go. The next generation of problem resolution dynamics represents a mental product of significant exponential resource for humankind. The software for this new thinking modeling extends from an absolute core shift removing the virus of competitive thinking permitting the master manifesting power of cooperation to shine through. Better decisions, more frequent decisions, higher quality decisions all of the time. A resolution dynamic of cooperation impossible to equal when competitive limitations are applied. Cooperation reformers are revolutionaries of the NOW kind– and are working tirelessly, creating and leading teams to effect future outcome.

Competition represents a failed mathematical model as an organizing principle for human affairs. Those who guard, protect and perpetuate a broken thinking model of competition solution dynamics, (primarily due to educational programs they open and operate without knowing who loaded the original software) – retard Global Progress. SNAP is such a visibly "better way" of moving quality and performance into the future, even die-hard competitionalists tend to "give it up" once they experience SNAP as a better way. The proof is always in the doing. SNAP is a do-it-now mindset. SNAP is a progressive mental elevator for reforming your thinking process forward into improved quality. SNAP is a cooperative technology impossible to apply in a competitive structure. Competitive organizations are dying. Cooperative organizations are thriving. Reforming corporate systems into cooperative futures is the primary mission of retraining for the coming centuries. A fact that applies to all institutions from a one-person, home-based business, to industry, to governments. Leaders will want to KNOW. Leaders will want to know HOW. Leaders will want to know NOW. Leaders will want to adopt a "better way." Cooperation is the better way resolution dynamic for all human organizing systems forward of the time in which we now reside.

Massive upgrades in performance rely on the old principle......who you know in life counts. No longer is the closed circle of a privileged alumni contact base adequate to propel innovation and evolution of the human experience. The global village is a cooperative enterprise of many minds in collaboration. Cooperation rules apply. SNAP is a leading example of cooperative technology. SNAP evolves cooperation, as a proven model, into the forward communication age technology of "who you know; and who they know; and who they know through six clicks of separation" delivering increasingly higher performance effecting even more people in less time.

Key affiliations can warp drive higher forms of productivity in society. SNAP students will wish to keep in mind "who you know" is a **renewable** resource. Each of us can retrain in the crucial area of systems modeling to cultivate the most important organic garden of "mind" by fertilizing God's richest soil for decision-making – via an enlarged process of NETWORKING that we have trademarked SUPER NETWORKING. SNAP is a visible technology. Before SNAP one would order a product or service and wait perhaps 90 days for delivery. After SNAP the world is moving toward an online, hand-held, anytime, order-for-service process in which the delivery may be as low as 90 minutes – perhaps, in the future, 90 seconds. SNAP. Ask your teams, "Is it SNAPPED yet?" – meaning how many minds have plussed and improved value to any proposed execution concept in 90 seconds or less. If you don't have a mental picture of what SNAP technology looks like – you are a candidate for cooperation experiential retraining. Once you experience hands-on, CEO-to-CEO performance gains from the better way of cooperative versus competitive system modeling – you'll move to reform your core system dynamic. A better way always wins! CEO leaders can adopt no higher form of time use value than to manufacture cooperation into their core systems sooner rather than later.

Leadership retraining on the topics of cooperation systems and SUPER NETWORKING induce rapid performance gains for any work environment or society where such skills are applied, regardless of size of institution served. Cooperation always works better wherever it is applied. Teams using SNAP principles begin to out-perform teams failing to learn and apply SNAP technology as a solution engine. Those who apply SNAP technology flourish. Decades of research and applied interaction have led to next generation systems modeling for Government and private industry in applied cooperation retraining. Cooperation WORKS ~ Super Networking WORKS. The global village is built upon these two new principles. Mastering them is a CEO mandate.

Networking is the skill of the decade....the skill too few graduates from conventional education presently understand....nor can they acquire SNAP skills from conventional training based upon an antiquated, failed competitive modeling technology.

CEO TIP: Leaders and their core teams might spend the time and allocate investment resources to use SNAP (our acronym for 21st century networking technology) as a priority for upgrades to yesterday's performance software (training). Seek out and attend better corporate trainings, drawing upon this cornerstone topic to rapidly reprogram your core team and internal systems. Embrace SNAP team-to-team problem solving. Investing to UPGRADE your "system" software yields the higher returns on time and resources. Ask corporate trainers what cooperation and SNAP training they are offering – acquire a multi-year process training product versus an event driven, single event training service.

Super Achiever Mindsets is the ultimate encyclopedia for the Leader politically or for the CEO reformer who seeks to apply time and resources more wisely to the leadership process in business and in life. As such, *Super Achiever* produces two results in support of tomorrow's planet shifting leaders. First, *Super Achiever* is a social transformation publication that provides the vocabulary of our rapidly evolving Global Village economic state. Second, *Super Achiever* defines the tools required to fly from the bridge of this new Global Village "financial" community, serving political and CEO leaders who wish to assume command.

SNAP technology (a federally trademarked system, coined by the author) seeks to help retrain "cooperative" leaders moving into global village command...to reshape the way leaders think....to help global leaders install upgrades to judgment software when making future decisions....to upgrade priority choice software - until your decisions conclude: "THIS becomes more important than THAT" as a natural Super Achiever mind process known as discernment/reflection – and the missing leadership CORE skill: Decision reformation training....the technique to apply SUPER ACHIEVER decision-making to all resolution mapping-executing the work product DECISIONS using - SNAP or

Super Networking Accelerates Potential – as the warp drive motor to move Decisions into REALITY with higher quality and greater speed. Tomorrow's leaders are tuned in to the need for the software program upgrades of the mind for themselves and their core teams.

Leadership is a unique way of thinking. Leadership is a "learned behavior and anyone can learn it." Super Achiever mindsets represent a conditioned training of mind by choice rather than by accident. Mental discipline is the first and most important state of acquiring Super Achiever skill. Everyone is "not" born with a Super Achiever mindset. Not everyone from traditional environments and, even through mentorship, acquires the mental software of the Super Achiever mindset. If human potential is the most valuable of all earthly assets, then reprogramming humanity to adopt Super Achiever mental software may be the priority mission of our human future. The computer of the mind does operate with multiple viruses that affect the end product. The user/operator often does not know his system is operating slower and with errors. Removing viruses of the mind is the responsibility of TEAM LEADERS who are elevating team "like mindedness" toward common Super Achiever mindsets.

Super Achiever software loading and operation is a learned behavior. Any hardware (human being) can learn to load and operate Super Achiever software. The first step to doing so is to acknowledge that "better code" is available and to DECIDE as a future leader – you wish to acquire better code for the software of your own mind – every time upgrades for such software become available. Super Achievers have checked the option for AUTO UPGRADES – ON and their acquisition of new mental software (via frequent training) is historic. Better trained mental computers operate with virus-free, upgraded software and perform better individually and in groups.

Setting better priorities is a condition of mind that produces higher alertfulness to the decision process through INTERVEN-TION. Making better decisions is a science of human awareness known as retraining. Networking exercises (retraining) are the ultimate wake-up call to conscious thinking in the fabric of today's global village lifestyles. By associating with Super Achiever mindsets, your own pattern of problem solving is transformed. Humans learn by doing. Humans learn by copying. Better mental software is best redistributed at its highest quality and bandwidth and via its most compressed form, known as MENTORSHIP. Mentorship is always high bandwidth and frequently wireless. If a receiver's mailbox is full however, the incoming may be forever lost.

Too many leadership decisions are made while we are virtually asleep running habitualized software vs. making higher quality decisions with OS "inside" drawing upon humanity's most awake operating Super Achiever Mental Software. Electing to quality control every decision to assure each choice has RE-FLECTION and INTERVENTION entwined like a magic DNA code to the core choices of Judgment for the moment-to-moment requirements of leadership, produces JUDGEMENT in the Decision Process. Judgment is a display of more awareness for consequence to individual executions. Judgment represents a habitual split-second of priority reflection as to which choice comes first; which flows next; which choice flows not at all; often making all the difference in the world for team or individual results. Leader Question: Can you hire a core team whereby you KNOW in advance each teammate has maximum judgment? Can you? How? What would be the value of quality control over KNOW-ING the relative judgment skill your team or a key person offers without "seeing" their output over time? How valuable to your team would the quality control be to know that your entire team embraced Super Achiever mindset principles from this moment forward, as a software maintenance prime directive and as mental quality control in your work environment? Begin to place values on the mental software of your team, first as the source of all output – and your measurement of throughput second, as the consequence or symptom the mental STATE created by your organizing principles.

Networking is not just about contacts. Networking is not just about opportunity. Cooperative Networking is a PROCESS OF MIND that delivers the goods of SUPER ACHIEVER decision-making every day team leaders are in "command." I know. I've seen George Bush (senior) in action in his prime. I've watched his son, in his prime. In this top leadership job, the Super Achiever mindset becomes the cornerstone upon which the core team is maintained.

George Bush is both a Super Achiever and a SNAPPER...a SUPER NETWORKER!

The President knows the rules of the Global Village Game.

MY LIFE, THE MOVIE

Readers like to know a little bit about their authors. I take my own story as a comedy rather than a serious adventure. My SNAP story is, however, consuming.

My life, the movie, is complex. Some Hollywood producers are discussing making a drama of my life story, and I may have to endure it. Hopefully, they'll politely wait until I pass. I'm sure they'll dwell more on my challenges and failures than on the periods I've operated Global companies. In the end, the movie will be what many remember about "my life." While living it, I submit the only thing that matters about anyone's life is "what comes next." Everything else is a memory and has no value. However, to satisfy some of my reader's curiosity (the rest can scan past it):

I was born Bernhard Joseph Dohrmann to Alan and Marjorie Dohrmann at Saint Mary's Hospital in San Francisco. My father, Alan Dohrmann, was born at Saint Mary's Hospital in San Francisco. My grandfather, for whom I was named, was born in Saint Mary's Hospital in San Francisco. My great grandfather was born in San Francisco, but Saint Mary's wasn't yet built. His father was the son of the Surgeon General to the King of Denmark at the time. A far too self-confident, young whipper snapper who made the DECISION to leave the King's court, as a Baron of Germany, a rare teen of royal blood, Grandfather Dohrmann booked his passage on a sailing ship to the gold fields, landed on San Francisco's Barbary Coast after a very rough number of months on the high seas. The Barbary Coast during the gold rush years was about as far from the civility of the King of Denmark's court, as the Baron son to the King's surgeon could travel. He wanted to make his mark on the new world and his own way in the future he imagined free of the Dohrmann wealth and legacy. He wanted to make it on his own.

He didn't make it unscathed. Instead he slipped, on a stormy night on a ship's slippery wet plank as the waves broke over a challenged bow, and broke his arm. Young Dohrmann off-loaded in the real Wild West at the bright age of seventeen, with wooden splints from the ship's carpenter taped with rags around his slow-to-heal arm. His surgeon father would not have approved.

The sights and smells of gold fever in San Francisco in the 1800's were far from the elegance of the King's kitchens back home in Denmark, and even a scrap of bread was a luxury for the one-armed nobility. Young Dohrmann quickly found class and heritage represented a never-ending ridicule in this place called America, where all were known by their deeds not their pedigree. Money was pouring into the transcontinental railroad, and the horse and buggy still ruled the unpleasant transportation of humans, only slightly challenged by the occasional loud and stinking horseless carriages. The hills of San Francisco were being conquered by a new technology known as Cable Cars. The young man had no construction jobs available to him, with only the use of one arm.

My greatest grandfather did some magic to convince a hardware store owner to allow the one-armed boy to clean some ancient ship's brass stored upstairs. Granddad was a genius in marketing which a surprised, lumberjack hardware store owner was about to discover. In one week, the newly shined brass was gone, and the store profits were up for the month. In one year, the eighteen year-old was a partner. A short time later, he owned the store....and a decision was made.

Granddad decided that going up into the gold fields, with all the fuss, was only one method to strike it rich. ABC Dohrmann had connections. Networks of connections. Important Connections. In Denmark. In Germany. His father was an important man, a titled gentleman which carried weight even on the Barbary Coast of California. Kings and Barons held sway over the imagination of a new country still testing its mettle.

Grandpa Dohrmann developed a VISION. He saw a future where instead of prospecting and working with the unlikely "beat the odds" hope against hope of actually unearthing a great gold find, he would strike another form of mother load. In the income-tax-free days of early America, Grandpa Dohrmann conceived of a personal VISION, a method to tax each and every ounce of gold and participate by keeping just a little of the American dream from each one.

INNKEEPER Dohrmann saw the future with perspective. The future along the budding railroad and highway tracks of America - Innkeeping. Millions of dreamers were importing their dreams from Europe, from Asia, from Africa and elsewhere. Everyone was on the move or so it seemed. Everyone required lodging. Hotels, motels, way-stations and INNS had to BE the future....and all the budding INNS needed supplies.

Each new Inn needed linens from Europe, crystal glasses from Denmark, towels from Holland and kitchenware and hardware from his father's factories in Germany. YES! He could see the future and the future was NETWORKING.

The story becomes another book which I am letting my brother

Geof create. The summary version leads to my immediate grandfather, Albert Bernhard (my namesake) Charles Dohrmann, a man with twelve children, of which my father was the last set of twins. He and his brother, Jerry, ruled the roost as babies.

There was no depression for the family that founded the Saint Francis Hotel; helped make Yosemite a national park; invented the famous Emporium department store chain; and managed one of the largest resort outfitting companies in the world, DOHRMANN Hotel Supply. Father grew up in private schools and the family business.

For most of my father's life (Alan Gerard Dohrmann) he wrote course material in what is now known as simply: THE MIND BUSINESS. Eighty billion dollars a year or so, by 1993, estimated to exceed 120 Billion a year by 2004, an industry built upon putting the new sciences of human behavior into our brains so that we can use our lives more productively.

Dad raised his nine children, Terry, Pam, Sally, Susan, Carl, Mark, Geof, Melissa and me, from a soap box. We all look back and smile at the lessons and practice sessions this great teacher employed, testing his latest courses out on US. From the Catholic Church, to the greatest companies and individuals in the human performance industry, Alan Dohrmann was known for leadership - leading courses, leading classes, leading instruction in helping people gain empowerment.

The first time I saw Dad give out his business card, I was seven - blond hair, blue eyes and curious. Dad turned the card over to a fellow airline passenger. The card was very simple with no information about address, phone number, etc. The card simply said:

Alan Dohrmann
Artist

I never forgot my father's reply to the follow-up question, "Mr. Dohrmann, what type of art do you create?" Dad slid the glasses a bit down his nose as he looked up with the smile only an elf could possess and said, "Why, I specialize in self-por-traits."

THE SUMMARIES

SNAP is about Networking. I learned Networking from the greatest teachers....from my father, the human behaviorist pioneer and course designer....from his friends who developed the Mind Industry as we know it today.

And from the graduates of Dad's classes who captain many companies and leading organizations.

These lessons helped me associate with resort development projects when I was a teenager speaking on stage with Peter Uberoth, former Baseball Commissioner and producer of the Los Angeles Olympic Games.

Networking lessons helped me consult many of the greatest mind development companies in the world, companies such as Dr. Lee Pulos' *Adventures in Learning*, the late Val Van de Wall's *Xoces Western*, Jane Willhite's *PSI World*, and Greg Bungay's *Lifestyles* to name a few.

Networking helped me win a reputation first as a good and ultimately as a GREAT course designer. Dad passed in 1983 before he was able to see the results of his oldest son's performance in the market he helped found. He used to toast my success in the corporate world at Christmas galas and annual conventions saying, "This is my son, in whom I am well pleased." He lived to see that before I was thirty, I had failed and faced great challenges. He also saw me succeed in unparalleled success before and after success. Legends are built from the teeth of such stories. He saw my companies employ more than ten thousand employees, with sales of $50,000,000 a month, operating in fourteen countries with brochures in seven languages.

I always felt if I could succeed, against odds most people would shudder to face, ANYONE and I mean ANYONE can win success. Through the lessons of my life, I discovered that SUCCESS is a LEARNED behavior. Anyone with the time and the desire can learn to win.

While you are reading my book, I hope you develop a burning desire to change your results. If you are a multi-million dollar success story, I suggest your passion re-ignite to finale with even more grand and bold frontiers. If you are just starting out, I suggest you open your heart and dare to dream the great dream.

For over a decade I have helped to develop the leading courses being taught to human beings on the subject of Success....for corporate success in the boardroom....for relationship success in the family room....and for individual success in the largest room in the universe - the gymnasium of your mind - the room of human imagination.

Success IS a learned behavior.

In recent years I have operated advanced human potential training classes on the subjects of Income Acceleration, Relationships, Corporate Vision and Productivity Training and Mind Skills training.

THINK AND GO NOWHERE

Think and Go Nowhere is what's wrong with the mind business this minute. A human life is far too precious to waste. Time is life. There is only one factor about a Super Achiever that is different - the process the Super Achiever uses to make a decision, a choice, to set a priority. The *Super Achievers* MIND PROCESS is more awake than a non Super Achiever. For the remainder of this book, I will use the word YOU to equate to a Super Achiever, for example purposes.

I want YOU to think like a Super Achiever thinks. A 3% to 5% shift in the way your mental process works when you make a decision can improve the results you achieve in life by 300%, 500% and more. Learn how to increase the wakefulness of the process you use to make a decision.

Recent studies indicate that we have learned in the last twenty years 600% more than we knew about human behavior and the mind than was published or known in the entire framework of human history. Another way of looking at this issue is to consider that all the papers written on the mind and human behavior could have fit inside the national Library of Congress from the year 8000 BC until 1983.

From 1983 until today the new papers that have been written and published about the mind would fill all the library storage for all the libraries in all the countries of the world and still require 600 plus new libraries the size of the Library of Congress to contain these fresh publications. The pace of new information on the subject of the mind is accelerating.

How does this information become useful? How can the information be packaged so that an average person can put the information to work in his or her life? Even the experts are having trouble keeping up.

Consider: for decades we studied BIG. We studied the ocean and mapped the continents. Mankind focused attention on new empires, new lands, new worlds, even space. Man bent his mind to study big. Only in the past generation has man begun to study small.

With the atom, science learned there is more space in the human body than there is solid matter. No matter how small man goes, there is still smaller yet to discover.

Man now studies the firing of electric currents within the brain. We are opening one lock of our genetic code at a time. We focus on the secrets of thought and of life. We study and measure things today for which the hardware and software did not exist two years ago.

Startling, marvelous discoveries are being uncovered like the richest veins of ore. New knowledge that will help mankind emerge into the new dimension of life where Freedom and Liberation are the rule rather than the exception.

Some of the things we know about human behavior, that fall under the control of every individual, seem to surprise people. This same information will also Empower people....help people. Discovering this new information is powerful....important.

In the past, early mind publications noted the truths that:
- You create your own reality.
- To think is to create.

- You can be anything you desire to be.

The accent was on CAN. Students of the first generation of mind information had primitive guidelines for implementation of the CAN aspect of performance. Teachers who studied these disciplines noted that most people attempting to follow the guidelines did not change future results. Students tried. Students worked hard. Students listed goals. Students wrote affirmations.

The overwhelming data suggested that students did not alter future performance. Students did not experience success from their effort. In the process students would become frustrated. Students lacked sufficient new information to know WHY they weren't WINNING.

The key to the learned behavior of success is transforming the PROCESS for making a choice. This process is subtle. The procedures for improving the thinking process are known as PROCESS TECHNOLOGIES.

Students who master the techniques of Process Technology will learn:

- You can achieve the result you envision in the time you set.
- Specific instruction on WHAT steps to take to win.
- Specifics on HOW TO take each step toward new success and in what sequence the steps should be taken.
- Ongoing support that will assure the student will not fail or backslide on his or her progress toward improved Process and Success.

Until recently, first generation mind instruction has focused upon EVENT TECHNOLOGY. The student acquired a book. The student purchased a series of tapes. The student attended a seminar. The information was event driven. The Event started and the Event stopped. As time passed the student was disappointed because insufficient tools to change process, and hence develop successful life patterns, were imparted. The results the student experienced remained largely unchanged. This condition produces frustration, fear and disillusionment.

Think and go nowhere became the rule rather than the exception to twenty years of mind instruction.

Seminar availability for the topic of self-improvement exploded. Students can now attend thousands of different seminars on mind subjects. Seminars have proven useful only as "introductory" tools.

Seminars introduce students to a large body of important new information about the mind sciences industry. However, seminars have proven to be relatively ineffective as personal empowerment technologies. Seminars do not transfer new MIND PROCESSES to the individual. New Skill to make better decisions is typically not installed following the completion of a seminar program. Seminars are LITE INSTRUCTIONS, like Bud Lite or Miller Lite. No calories, no mental weight is taken on. Students remain the same LITE WEIGHTS they were before the SEMINAR. A heavy weight PROCESS SYSTEM was increasingly in demand by the early 1990s.

Consider that you enrolled in a classroom to learn to fly. On Wednesday you would fly five hours with a live instructor in a morning. Imagine approaching this strange and wonderful machinery called an airplane....reviewing all of the control surfaces, as yet so unfamiliar, studying the panel of strange dials and instruments - feeling more than overwhelmed. But you proceed to complete your morning flying lesson. You then go on and schedule a late afternoon flying lesson. You decide to spend the rest of the day in ground "school" learning the theory and basics of flight. You would repeat this study each day – Thursday, Friday, Saturday and Sunday. By Sunday you would have over thirty hours of instructor flying time. You would have practiced real flying in your classroom of flight each day, morning and afternoon.

Late Sunday afternoon, prior to sunset, your instructor would give you the airplane keys. You would meet all FAA FAR regulations to actually FLY solo. You would enter your airplane, a plane you first flew a few days ago. You would taxi, take off and return. You would pick up your radio and say skillfully, "Tower this is niner, niner Zulu turning on Final, request clearance for landing" as if you had done it forever. You would have enjoyed the transfer of a skill through the auspices of a class.

If you had attended a SEMINAR on flight, sat in the classroom, and completed the seminar in the same time frame, you would know all the benefits of flying. You would know a great deal about flying. However, on Sunday afternoon, NO ONE (and I mean NO ONE) would get into the airplane with you!

A hands-on class will transfer skill that you can reproduce and put to work in your life. A class on desktop publishing will empower you to take the disks home and perform the desktop publishing on your home computer. Complete a CLASS on flying and YOU WILL FLY!

If the student wishes to master a new mind skill, the only proven method is to explore a class that will transfer the skill you seek to obtain. Results are **UN-likely** to change for most people on any subject when a seminar is the method of instruction chosen. Seminars are useful **introductory** tools. Increasingly students seek out PROCESS TECHNOLOGY classes. Process Technology education can be purchased from hundreds of companies for the same price as a seminar. Why go for the finish line without a winning horse? Play it smart while on the track of life.....bet forever. There is no return match folks. This IS your adulthood, not a dress rehearsal. Go for the roses NOW and don't look back.

Success is waiting for you to discover. After all, your personal success has simply been waiting for you to WAKE UP and enjoy the experience.

BASICS TO REMEMBER

A class is a skill transfer technology. The best classes provide after-graduation support.

Think and go nowhere is wasteful to life.

Think and go nowhere is a habit. It's a habit every individual can break. To discover successful thinking patterns one must learn. There is no instant learning, however there is accelerated learning in this information age. Investing time and money to develop successful MIND PROCESS is the most important priority in life. Shift other priorities to lesser importance. The decision is yours. The choice can be made in a SNAP!

Think and go somewhere is a destination every student must begin.

BRAINSTORM...
PASSKEY TO FAILURE

Who you know is simply crucial to success. In developing success for so many of my students we have hit on a number of formulas which appear to work for everyone - the housewife with no real business interest or experience....the multimillionaire who has earned millions of dollars EACH and EVERY year for the past eight years in a row....the singer....the author....the inventor....the healer....the lawyer....the executive....those professions supporting all of us in labor industries - those who want to BECOME the manager of their own destiny instead of supporting a Manager controlling "them."

I learned this secret from Dr. Mark Victor Hansen, best-selling futurist, speaker and Fortune 500 Company trainer, author of *Chicken Soup for the Soul*. Mark insisted I look at his concept. His idea formed after looking over the systems for MAINTAINING wealth used by 100% of his contacts that ran the largest Fortune companies.

I went to visit Mark in 1988 and spent some time at his home in Newport Beach. In-between playing with his two beautiful blonde daughters, Melanie and Elizabeth, I learned the secret to wealth building every one of my students could discover.

Mark pointed out his research demonstrated ALL wealthy people earned income from more than one source. All wealthy people earned income from two, three, five and sometimes a whole lot more separate income sources.

Mark also completed my education by alerting me to the specific TRUTH that wealthy people did not view these MULTIPLE INCOME SOURCES as J.O.B.s. Rather wealthy people regarded the idea, the concept of earning income from numerous sources a "technology" - Multiple Income Technology.

Also, I discovered that ALL wealthy people employ Multiple Income Technologies to sustain their wealth. Multiple Income Technologies follow specific patterns or rules which include:

- You must be passionate about the Multiple Incomes you choose.
- The Multiple Incomes must never, ever interfere with your primary source of income.
- The Multiple Income Source must earn income for you in a short time frame, say eight to twelve weeks.
- It must continue to earn income for you for years.
- It must not interfere with balance in your life.

To send a Multiple Income Technology into orbit every aspiring millionaire must first select one to work on. You don't have to think up the idea yourself. Again, who you know is the secret ingredient. Everyone can fall in love with an idea. The idea of hot pizzas delivered to your home created a billion dollar industry. The idea of a new service, the idea of some new artistic product, for that matter any idea becomes the power plant. The IDEA is the asset. Every job, every company, every product, every service, every item you feel, see or touch began as an IDEA, a thought, either in someone's mind or in God's.

If you don't have an idea that fills your life with PASSION, don't worry about it. Don't become anxious. All that is required is you WANT such an idea. An idea that you say "Oh, I am so glad to rise this morning and play with this idea that is going on in my life...I am so grateful for IT!"

Such an idea is based in PASSION you and you alone possess....a love for something creative, a DREAM you hold onto in your heart, a dream you will never ever give up on. Passion makes life more meaningFULL......lack of passions in life make life more meaningLESS. To increase your meaning in life you must assume the risk of adopting an idea that delivers PASSION into your world. Dreams are what we live for. Without them life becomes a motion hardly worth going through.

I can't define the renewal I have seen from men and women of all walks of life, when they discovered a new PROCESS for adopting passion back into their life. When the focus is on making multiple sources of income, the pleasure of the passion is even more inviting as the consequence is financial expression and freedom.

Selecting an idea is easier than you might think. Everyone thinks of ideas that might work. Everyone reading this book has said to themselves "Why that guy's making a mint on an idea I thought up a while back"... or "I know I could make that idea work" or "I wish I had thought of that".... etc.

Everyone can love an idea.

Everyone can move an idea into a money-making Multiple Income Stream. You just have to watch for the opportunities. In conversations everywhere there are more ideas than there are fertile minds to undertake them. Keep your mind receptive.

Remember: nothing but nothing grows on fields of ice! The tundra is not conducive to your mental health. Grow new ideas in the tropics. Plant your ideas in fields open to suggestion.

Move your self-talk from "Why we can't" to "HOW WE WILL." Monitor the inventory of your thoughts like a clerk in a library. Clear your thoughts to blank once in a while and rest. Then, begin again. Shout SWITCH when your mind is dishing up the "Why-we-can't" thoughts on any subject, and teach others in teams, groups and families to SWITCH as well. Every mind can elevate its process for file clerk thought control in the most important of all work performed during a state we call AWAKE in a place we call LIFE.

Discover that you can and will become successful. Insist that latent talent you have within you is free to emerge. Do something you have always loved to do.

How many of us wanted to move in a specific direction but fate put us in a more practical (we thought) track. Mother said "Be a doctor, be a lawyer...make something of your life." Maybe you hated science classes or Latin. But you had to proceed toward the idea of "making it big." Now, maybe you hate your job.

Say you do hernia surgery - procedure number 2911. You do procedure 2911 pretty well. You get up at 5:30 A.M. You go to the little hospital room....have some coffee....read something....make small talk to the anesthesiologist you share fees with. You put on the green shoes and the green hat. You scrub.

You move on to perform procedure number 2911. In fact, you perform the procedure eight times that day....many days, just like you have for the past ten years. Yes....you have prestige. Yes....you have money. You DO get phone calls at odd hours. You DO have trouble getting any real time off. You DO have a kind of bondage to your procedures. Your time is not your own. True....your life is often not your own. True....you give up so much of your family and social life to the whims of nature and complete strangers.

AND you may not LIKE your J.O.B. very much ten years

later. You may never have liked your J.O.B. Sometimes you may catch yourself considering that even a butcher gets more variety. At least they get pork and fowl once in awhile. All you get is the beef!

A BETTER WAY

There is a better way. It can start with something as simple as an idea you are warming up to, a new idea for a Multiple Income Source (MIS) you want to develop into a full blown MIS, a technology for making income. Income that may double, triple or quadruple your current income. Income that is NOT another JOB. Income that is FUN to think about. Income that is YOU!

"But how? Oh, how?" you may lament, can you discover the right idea for you.

First let's set some more success guidelines into place:
- Choose only one idea at a time.
- Choose an idea you can fall in love with.
- Develop a practical plan to make the idea win and win big.
- If you don't succeed with your first plan, develop a second plan and a third plan.
- Remember - your idea, once selected, is perfect. Only your plan may need improvement.

You now have some ideas for how to proceed to develop a MIS. You next need to develop a support team to help you...a like-minded support team, a positive support team. In fact, a far more positive team than you may have selected previously - at any prior time in your life.

You will require new skill to select this superior team. No wealthy, successful person arrived at his exalted position without a powerful support team. The support team typically is a well-organized MASTERMIND.

MASTERMIND THE PRINCIPAL

A Mastermind team is comprised of two to seven individuals who are like-minded, in agreement and committed to create project solutions for definite purposes and missions established by the team. Every great leader talks and writes about his Mastermind.

A Mastermind is a formal, highly-organized activity between like-minded individuals. A Mastermind Team is not typically:

- A brain-storming session
- A general session
- A random session

A Mastermind is selected because of the BLEND of skill and talent each team member brings to the team. Mastermind Teams can be developed to assist individuals to succeed with any life project. Tasks may include relationships with children, life partners, career partners or choices, lifestyle plans, success planning, goal attainment, retirement, education, self improvement or any number of topics established by the team leader.

A Mastermind can be a loose brainstorming session, when the Mastermind has no team leader and no defined mission to work on. Brainstorming sessions are fun, but almost always useless.

Brainstorming Mastermind Teams have been the rule in virtually all publications on the subject until the dawn of SUPER NETWORKING. Why? No one had a rule book for developing new MIND PROCESS. New data published about the mind provides proof positive success can be learned by everyone. The already successful can elevate outstanding processes to even sharper, more highly-focused results.

Brainstorming does not alter the PROCESS for making a decision. New MIND SKILL has not been learned. Mastermind Teams that are BRAINSTORMS are fun. The lightning still flies. The rain of ideas still flow and those involved feel GOOD....even GREAT. However, for the most part, results in life do not change with a Brainstorming Mastermind Team. Something MORE is required. But what?

A Mastermind is a powerful force when the team is highly organized, led with clarity by a team leader and in agreement to resolve specific missions. Napoleon Hill stated in *Think and Grow Rich* that Mastermind sessions should be convened twice weekly. Why?

Mastermind sessions are one of the only known exercises for the muscle of the mind. Mastermind Sessions develop a heightened state of awareness - a state of awareness so advanced that the effects are felt for many days after the session is completed. The PROCESS of thought itself is altered and improved through exercise. Improved further through repetition.

The PROCESS of becoming more awake to the selective ACTION of making a Decision with elevated use of JUDGEMENT skill is derived as a benefit from Mastermind Team sessions. Mastermind Team sessions exercise the mind to stimulate an improved PROCESS for SUPER ACHIEVER Decision patterns.

Years of research and study in all developed countries of the world have concluded some important findings the public is slow to recognize:

- What is MOST unique about *Super Achievers* on a global basis is what is THE SAME about the way they think.
- What is the SAME about the way ALL *Super Achievers* THINK is the superior PROCESS they employ to set priorities, make decisions and employ judgment when choosing.
- *Super Achievers* ALL live life as pro-active, agenda-setting human beings as opposed to RE-ACTIVE automated thinkers (or unconscious decision-makers).
- The Super Achiever lifestyle (success) is a LEARNED behavior.

Everyone can learn to THINK like a Super Achiever. The mind science of discovery that leads to Super Achiever Lifestyles is a science devoted to changing the PROCESS of making CHOICES by only a slight degree. With a tiny change to the PROCESS of making a choice, an individual can alter results achieved in life by 300%. The effects are immediate.

The goal is to foster a more wakeful condition to making choice. To be more alert to the policy decisions that each one of us make each and every day. To tap into the unlimited MIND POWER that is hiding inside each one of us.

But HOW?

The process, once begun, is hard to reverse. Once an individual wakes up from the sleep of lazy decision-making, it is hard to return to a symbolistic state of living. The alert and awakened individual will fight to retain the wakeful condition of mind attained.

Success IS a learned behavior. Success unfolds from regular repetitive workout of the most important muscle of your body, your mind!

BUT HOW?

First, realize you probably won't succeed if you try to win your new wakeful condition by yourself. Life is too heavily conditioned with sleepy thinkers. The circle of mediocrity that surrounds each of us will sweep you to sleep before you know it's happening.

We each make countless choices each day without any idea why, how or even THAT we made them. We simply allow our power plant, our mind, to run largely out of control....by habit. Waking up separates us to some degree from mediocrity. We become somewhat more excellent....somewhat more outstanding....somewhat brighter.

Major corporations are investing tens of millions of dollars for classrooms that will help their best resources, their people, to WAKE UP. A more wakeful work environment alters performance more than all the investments in plant, robotics and high technology combined. Process Technology education is a tax-benefited investment in self - the selfness of the individual, the self of the corporation. The results of "wake-up-call" education can be staggering. Success, once learned, is such a pleasure no one wishes to return to a lower state of awareness.

Our friends and family may not applaud this brighter outlook, however. In fact, they may try pretty darn hard to get you back into the circle of mediocrity - the circle they think you belong in, the circle they feel comfortable with, the circle they plan for you to sit in for the rest of your life.

Waking up can be avoided to enjoy the status quo. Success is not the status quo. Don't expect everyone to applaud your efforts to become successful. Many will not. Arranging support teams around your life is part of the hard work of exercising the muscle of your mind.

You are not just trying to WIN and WIN BIG. You are trying to WIN and WIN FOR CERTAIN!

If you are like the great majority of people, you do better at exercising any muscle in a gym, with a group or team, with some organized activity. Remember: your mind IS a muscle. It's the most important muscle of your entire body.

For a long time you may have failed to exercise the muscle of your mind. Your mind may be more out of shape than you realize. Therefore, you may require regular ongoing exercise to put your mind into tip-top shape. The muscle of the mind never ever ages. The muscle of the mind is always young, always vital, always willing to excel. The muscle of the mind is eager to break old records. The muscle of the mind is the only muscle that can restore its complete fitness at any age, in only minutes. No other muscle regains its full potential as fast.

Again, if you're like most people you do best when challenged by a well-organized team. A MASTERMIND team.

The mind like any muscle responds to success. Winning at pull-ups makes you do even more. Winning at a race makes you run EVEN faster. Jogging a few miles makes you jog even further. Successful thinking rewards the mind in such a way that only more successful thinking will follow.

The magic is TO BEGIN!

Mastermind exercises are not brainstorms. Mastermind exercises are highly-organized functions that stimulate the most important muscle of the body, your mind. The purpose of Mastermind Exercises is to achieve SUCCESSFUL thoughts from your mind, by improving your PROCESS for making decisions.

The glow that comes from athletic workouts also occurs when the mind is exercised. The condition of successful mental workouts brings the mind to a heightened state known as AWAKE.

GETTING AWAKE AND STAYING AWAKE

Students with a passion to become successful should focus their attention on highly-organized activity. The only ingredients that create success are:

THE APPLICATION OF HIGHLY-ORGANIZED ACTIVITY AROUND SPECIALIZED KNOWLEDGE.

In the case of our preparing for SNAP EXERCISES (the first new exercise for the muscle of the mind in 100 years) we begin with Multiple Income Technology as the specialized knowledge. Business class exercises, modeled around developing one or more Multiple Income Sources to surround a Primary Source of ACTIV-ITY (career), stimulate solid plans for wealth building. This Process can be fun while benefiting the individual. Skill and talent are deployed at an accelerated pace.

ALL LASTING WEALTH IS DERIVED FROM SERVICE PRO-VIDED TO HUMANITY BY WELL-INTENDED, LIKE-MINDED INDIVIDUALS SEEKING TO BENEFIT OTHERS.

Your premise for generating success should center upon a desire to discover how you can apply known or hidden skills to benefit humanity. Search for opportunities to demonstrate how you can exploit rich talents you have within, develop new talents and stimulate existing talents. Always expand your sights. Keep your mind focused on how you WILL succeed. SWITCH any and all mental files that use old, out-dated programs of "Why you can't" to HOW YOU WILL behavior. Hold only HOW YOU WILL thoughts. Smile and frequently shout SWITCH inside your mind. SNAP is another ideal word to SNAP out of old conditioning. Simply scream it inside your mind at your old, unwanted thoughts - SNAP OUT OF IT!

And you WILL!

Without any idea of WHAT your Multiple Income idea might be, select a team of like-minded individuals. Choose the best thinkers you know, but choose only individuals you find are, in fact, "like-minded" with you....individuals who are willing to give and share, positive thinkers. Interview carefully. If you develop a poorly performing team, stop meeting with them. Form another team. Start over. Exploit your freedom to choose. Practice until your team is really serving and supporting you. You will know when the team is right. Everyone does!

Tell each one "I am forming a Mastermind Team, and I wonder if you would agree to serve and support me in my efforts to win success. My request is that you agree to provide a commitment to support me with your talent, your skill and energy by meeting once every _____ (day of week) for one hour to ninety minutes. I am requesting members of my team each commit to 120 days of time, after which I will replace team members who seek to be substituted."

"In return, I promise to develop a formula that will benefit each member of my team from the success I plan to achieve....."

"May I request that you say, 'YES' so that I may count on your commitment to be a member of MY TEAM?"

"I want and choose you.............."

People LOVE to help one another. We simply work better together, you know.

LIKE-MINDED LIVING

Most of us could use a big jolt of higher self-esteem - the stuff that makes us feel deserving, empowered, entitled, worthy....the fragile fragrance that makes us feel really good about ourselves. We feel better about us. We feel better about others. With HIGH SELF-ESTEEM we feel better about everything.

Low self-esteem is a global epidemic. Low self-esteem saps the life tar out of the Giant Sequoia Tree that is your spirit. Low self-esteem robs nations of the ability to stimulate direction by energizing vision into their equations for future success. Proverbs states, "A people without vision...perish." As in...DIE. People need vision. Individuals need vision. Families need vision. Nations need vision to lead to their destiny.

Low self-esteem grounds the power of mental creative effort. The spark of divinity within us is neutralized by low self-esteem. One word, one negative event, can develop feelings of victimhood, martyrdom, and blame....common success killers.

High self-esteem defeats success killers. Maintaining self-esteem is far easier within a support team.

SELF CHECK

Support item: Great OK Needs Improvement Awful

- How do your friends support you?

- How does your life partner support you?

- How do your career partners support you?

- How does your self-talk support you?

- How do your family members support you?

- How does your current life support you?

- How do your children support you?

- How do you support your own desires?

Think about the new success idea you are planning to develop. How will your existing teams support you?

Don't get too specific if you do not have an idea yet. Rather, focus on the absolute certainty you will be successful. See yourself living in the consequence of what success means to you. Visualize the events, the lifestyle, and the ingredients of success that would mean something to YOU. These ideas or visions will help you choose a path to achieve these ideas. Every "Why we can't" thought will be seen as an old habit, an old condition of mediocre thinking and will be SNAPPED into a more positive HOW WE WILL. Recognize "Why we can't" thinking as an illusion of mind, not reality. Throw such thoughts into the garbage. When?

In a SNAP!

Each of us is FREE to plan our team environment for maximum benefit. Never judge another human as negative, unworthy or bad. Only DECIDE one issue: Is the person I am listening to LIKE-MINDED with me on this particular subject.

One team may be like-minded with you on some subjects, but not on others. The same holds true for team members individually. However, your Mastermind Team must pledge to support you in a positive, encouraging, uplifting manner. You are about to travel at a new speed. The speed of thinking positively. You will need a new form of transportation. Your vehicle is a well-constructed Mastermind Team.

Many of us have teams that hold our history, our past, our entire background, and we love them for this depository of information and experience. However, these teams may be awful at supporting future choices we make, need....insist upon as we explore and grow.

Consider that corporations, like families and friends, hold the same team structure. Teams that can hold history and are useless to renew energy, passions and new creative direction. Refreshing such teams with new PROCESS TECHNOLOGY is key to our greater competitive victory in the market place of the 21st Century. We must stop learning from other cultures and start TEACHING them.

New teams must be developed. New teams must be selected with care. Be sensitive in your selection, always searching for individuals with like-minded agreement, like-minded support on the subject for which you chose the team. The Team may be one person or many persons.

Teams create exponential results. Two people working together do six times the mental performance of one person working six times as hard.

Your mind, when united with other minds, becomes a generator of incredible power. Obtaining like-minded support from your team is the beginning of a new process. A process that can't fail to lead you to the success you desire.

Team members selected for Networking represent a separate mission. Mastermind Teamwork is creative in nature. You are creating a new idea. You are creating priorities for HOW to tackle bringing the reality into existence. When you select teams for the purpose of preparing for SNAP exercises, seek individuals you KNOW are interested in achieving more success themselves...individuals you feel intuitively are givers, not takers....individuals you can relate to....individuals you feel will come together and work well with one another.

Remember: your goal is to form a like-minded, supportive, nurturing, positive-minded team. A team devoted to personal advancement, heightened wakefulness and Super Achiever lifestyles.

A Mastermind team may also function as a SNAP (networking) team. A networking team is working to develop contacts beneficial to your success. A Mastermind team is working to create priorities for action to deliver your success to you. Ask your Mastermind team members who will and who will not wish to also support you in Networking via SNAP Sessions soon to follow.

HISTORIC SUMMATION

After decades of studying the "small dimensions" within our minds, we have published more data than in all of human history. Up until recent years mankind was fascinated with the subject of BIG:

- Map the ocean floors
- Film the continent with infra-red from space
- Build the tallest building
- Engineer the longest tunnel

Today mankind is fascinated with SMALL. Take a picture of your liver cells. See the firing of the synapses in your brain. Discover how information is stored and retrieved within the mind.

New data learned only recently helps define the rules for success - success in any field. Success is now known to be a learned behavior. Anyone can learn to behave more successfully. Effort to gain and apply the new knowledge is required. Any person can make this effort.

A new exercise has been developed, one that creates new mental habits and works to replace old conditions within the mind. Old conditioning holds much of our existing mental inventory hostage to old performance. To retrain the mind to hold onto more elevated thoughts is a feature of ATTITUDE and COM-

MITMENT known as PROCESS TECHNOLOGY.

Success-driven individuals must aspire to successful behavior. Success-driven individuals must become emotionally involved with a passion to elevate their thought inventory. The tools to elevate thought inventory include:

- Awareness training by expert teachers
- PROCESS TECHNOLOGY for the decision-making process
- Daily exercise for the muscle of the mind
- Weekly team exercises for elevated awareness for priority management

The exercise of 21st Century Mastermind team meetings provides a basis that simply cannot fail to alter the decision process of an individual to a more elevated level of peak performance. The key to success lies in the effort of the individual to improve the PROCESS by which a series of decisions are made. It is not sufficient to KNOW the steps that should be taken, nor is it complete to begin to DO THE STEPS. What is required is to develop a new automated series of mental HABITS (new conditioning) that elevate the decision process....the technique of choice. The comfort zone for most individuals is to avoid any EFFORT that lifts awareness to the responsibility zone.

The responsibility zone is a condition of mind which provides the glimmer that a decision is being made and that personal review of the decision inventory is called for. This level of understanding is a far higher condition of mind than is customary. With this mental condition one can apply judgment to tease the day-to-day, minute-to-minute actions of the mind into higher performance. The skill involved is a MIND SKILL which, once mastered, will never leave you.

For most individuals, decisions are made through a largely unconscious, mysterious, automated process. The process involves conditions within the individual that cycle to balance desires with fears and anxiety to maintain COMFORT. Successful individuals challenge comfort until the feeling of discomfort becomes the normal feeling, a feeling of growth and liberation.

Fear is harnessed by successful thinkers through a process of control and action that propels performance.

Fear management is a learned behavior.

Most successful men and women began without any understanding of their process for making decisions.

Most successful men and women at some time had no money, no idea, no background, little or no education and no track record.

The great majority of successful men and women did not begin their journey toward success until after they reached the age of FORTY. Many started with a track record of repeated failure. Most had no formal upper education. Many had no money whatsoever. What changed, at age 40 plus, for the developing SUPER ACHIEVER?

What did they learn that you can discover?

Each learned a new method for making choice. A process of mind. A new habit for using mind skill to applications that improve results. If success IS a learned behavior, anyone and I mean ANYONE can learn more successful methods for achieving the results they truly desire. Let's get into the work, the meat and potatoes, of HOW one goes about retraining the MIND.

Successful men and women became emotionally involved with an idea. They developed plans (decisions) to surround making the idea a reality in their lives. They reset priorities (altered process). They learned from error and substituted their failed plans with new more successful plans. They never doubted their idea (dream) was perfect. Only their plans required improvement.

They worked regularly on their idea. They worked with increasing skill in organization until they became highly-organized. They developed specialized knowledge for the process of making decisions supportive to their idea. They obtained success from application of highly-organized efforts surrounding specialized knowledge (the idea or dream).

Napoleon Hill points out, in *Think and Grow Rich,* that the wealthy individuals of the world did not require that they possess wealth or the idea to begin. Today we know the magic that is required is the idea that every one of us can become emotionally involved with and the ability to seek out the money.

The idea may be a better relationship with our children. Or a new home. Or a new way to express our talents by obtaining multiple income from multiple sources. The idea may be career related or the idea may relate somewhere else in our life priority plan.

Think about the concept that 72% of all employment is developed from small independent business. Only 28% of all jobs, of all house payments, of all car payments, of all grocery bills, of all utility bills are paid for by the jobs provided by the MAJOR, larger companies.

Each of us could DO SO MUCH MORE if we would only become emotionally committed to independently creating a better life. Each of us CAN and MUST create a better life for ourself. The commitment to move ahead in life embellishes life for every other person on the planet earth to some degree. Anyone who sits on his/her skill and talent wastes the opportunity of a super future to some small degree. Everyone who rushes ahead to manufacture this better future enriches not only their own lives, but lights up the life of everyone else they touch. Everyone gains from positive decisions. Everyone benefits.

Everyone else is less than when we delay or pass. Everyone

else is more powerful and more OK when we commit and act. We feel more alive — because we ARE more alive.

The best tool to change results is the tool of forming and regularly meeting with Mastermind Life Success Teams, mastering modern networking and practicing the latest in more alert decision development. Like any great skill, stretching the mind to think successfully requires practice. Team support is required.

Everyone can learn the behavior of success. Everyone can learn the behavior of GREAT SUCCESS through practice.

The **method** is defined in the pages of SUPER ACHIEVER. You and only you can make the **decision** to try the new techniques.

Other earlier techniques did not work as well; or did not work all the time; or for everyone; or as fast. The new PROCESS TECHNOLOGY technique described in this publication DOES work for everyone and WILL work fast.

Success is a learned behavior. Everyone can live a brighter, more productive and fuller life. You will enjoy greater happiness, fulfillment and peace when you live your life as a SUPER ACHIEVER.

The remainder of this publication will tell you exactly HOW to become a Super Achiever, specifically WHAT steps you should take, in what sequence you should take these steps and what support you will require, when you put this book into a bookshelf, to assure you never EVER go back to the place you started from.

If you are wealthy today and you are reading these words, consider developing an order of magnitude explosion of the success you have right now. Challenge your skill. Maintain balance and work smarter not harder. Your market now is a global one. Your market tomorrow is an intergalactic market. Old paradigms WILL NOT guarantee the future you imagine. The past cannot assure reproduction of your results into tomorrow. Only imagination will guarantee success tomorrow. Imagination is the centerpiece of Mind Skill. Knowing what to do with it once you learn how to use it is living life as a SUPER ACHIEVER.

Provide ten times or even one hundred times the jobs and employment you provide today, if you're already wealthy and successful. Never stop your growth and expansion. NEVER! Life has no destinations. Life is a journey. There is no plateau in the living experience.

As a famous Russian philosopher stated about the human spirit, "All living creation either grows.....or it rots!"

If you are seeking to make your first fortune let nothing stand in your way. Erase the blackboard of your efforts to become wealthy. Start all over. Begin fresh.

Your FRESH START should begin this second. Don't look back. Look at the hourglass of decisions God has granted to you and know that each choice for your future falls like magic Diamonds, one decision at a time. Grab each new decision and make it the most special choice of your life.

Produce a future that contributes to a better standard of life for all human beings, in all countries. If you are reading this book in Tokyo or Frankfurt, Jerusalem or Paris, Cape Town or Rio, Abu Dhabi or London, New York or Vancouver, Moscow or Prague, you owe yourself success. You owe all of US your success.

Don't deny yourself!

Don't deny the rest of US!

The life of the Super Achiever is the correct and natural birthright of the aware and thinking human being who is the master of his or her universe.

MASTERMIND EXERCISES

The following rules will help you turn on and turn off a regular meeting with your Mastermind Team:

Set a date to begin. Make a list of prospective Team members you think would enjoy the PROCESS. Let them know it will be a fun time. Be enthusiastic. Expect some rejection and be insulated from any negative energy. Approach those you believe will be like-minded, positive supporters. Ask them simply: "Will you meet each week for 90 minutes with me to help me form a Mastermind Team to work on a project I think can bring more success into each of our lives? I have chosen you as one of my key mastermind team members. I will need some of your time, but it will be well worth the moments you invest into this opportunity for an improved future. Just say yes and meet with us at my home on _____at _____. Arrive early please and stay late. What's your answer YES or YES?"

1. Invite five to seven key people to join your Mastermind Team. Ask each individual to make a commitment to serve the team, to be like-minded with you, and to be supportive of the stated mission which you

share with each prospective member. Only bring like-minded members into the team. Start team meetings with three or more individuals in agreement.

2. Select individuals who can help you achieve your mission. You do not need to know the individual well. You may be introduced to the individual by others you know who understand the team mission and know key talent that can help.

3. State your mission (dream) clearly. Your team members should be sensible extensions of the mission personality. Know your objective. Your written statement must convey the idea with a WOW emotion that attracts others to the idea. Ask the best writer to help you phrase the idea. Dress your idea with words that convey the ideals and principals you empower into your dream, as well as the basic concept. Words are the clothing of ideals and dreams.

4. Establish a regular place and time to hold your Mastermind team meetings. All chairs are arranged in a CIRCLE. Refreshments are served before or after. The Meeting starts with the word GO following your introduction of purpose of THIS individual meeting. The meeting ends with the word END or COMPLETE. The meeting pauses with the word TIMEOUT or a raised hand which means silence and all debate ceases as all members raise their hands. This control language operates superior Team sessions. Memorize and practice.

5. Open your meeting by discussing your mission purpose and the priority you are working on for this specific meeting. If you do not have a priority to work on, then the purpose of the meeting is to create priorities for your Dream. Commercial projects generally require five areas of attention. For purposes of this publication, all Team functions are deemed to focus on the goal of doubling the personal income of the individual hosting the meeting, in six to eight weeks. The Team Leader is creating a secondary income source using MULTIPLE INCOME TECHNOLOGIES to develop new exciting income added to existing PRIMARY SOURCE OF INCOME.

- You must MAKE the service or product.
- You must CAPITALIZE the idea.
- You must ADMINISTRATE the idea.
- You must DISTRIBUTE the idea.
- You must MARKET the Idea.

6. The team must agree on a written statement of the mission statement for EACH meeting of a Mastermind team, known as the PURPOSE. To remain highly organized the meeting must remain ON PURPOSE. The team leader should allocate ten minutes maximum to the task of obtaining agreement and unanimous support for the mission statement as written. Meetings without a preamble that develops 100% agreement on a WRITTEN MISSION STATEMENT (purpose) for the individual meeting, dissipate 70% of the focused creative power of the meeting. If you have been a member of a Mastermind Team, recon-

nect and practice these rules. You will be amazed at the new RESULTS you will procure from the *same use of time.*

7. The team will then work on setting project priorities to fulfill the mission statement as written. Ideas for specific highly organized ACTION will be suggested and written down. One-half hour is devoted to creative function. Discover and organize action suggestions into priority, this comes first, that comes second and then the other thing comes next. Create a list. Then organize the list of "things that must be done to succeed."

8. The mastermind team will then be directed by the team leader to reorder the priorities of the ACTIONS suggested to complete the mission. The reordered priorities will be delegated to team members with appropriate skill. Time tables to complete the action will be established. Complete agreement by the team on the results of this effort is expressed for the final written statement of PURPOSE.

9. The Team may then spend remaining time networking (90 Minutes total - meeting must adjourn in 90 Minutes maximum..use alarm clock to end time). Key contacts helpful to the mission statement may be developed for the Team Leader or other members following up to the ACTION PLAN the team developed. Everyone should call and make appointments with Key Connections, right on the spot, helpful to the team leader. HOW WE WILL is the only mental

behavior permitted in Mastermind and Network Team activity.

10. Each new meeting is called to order after a discussion of the progress from the previous meeting and a statement by the leader of the suggested mission for the current meeting. The overview must consume no more than five minutes. The meeting is closed with a blessing. Ask that every team member be granted the most perfect possible future and attract the most perfect possible associations to share this future beside.

SUGGESTED BLESSING:

Lord, grant that every member of our mastermind team is empowered to use their talent and skill to attract the most perfect possible future into their lives, and to attract the most perfect possible partners to share this future into their lives. Amen.

The Blessing is given in a circle meeting with team members holding hands.

This exercise provides a HIGHLY ORGANIZED meeting flow. The exercise suggested provides accelerated results, derived from elevated decision-making PROCESS. These lessons are instructed and practiced in various advanced human potential training classrooms around the world. If you have the opportunity to invest the time and money to experience advanced forms of mastermind team education or network education, set other priorities aside and enroll into the next possible class. Never stop learning new skill to employ this ultimate exercise for the muscle of the mind. The experience of this exercise is a wake-up call for the sleepy muscle of the mind. A wake up call that works for everyone. Once awake, the mind muscle will never go back to sleep again. Invest whatever it takes to elevate the 3% to 5% added wakefulness to the Decision Process that guarantees your personal SUPER ACHIEVER lifestyle.

The Form of Mastermind Team operation suggested in this book was invented following five million dollars of experimental class instruction over a five-year period involving MANY of the leading Fortune 500 Company educators. The result is a highly perfected exercise for the mind, which produces measurable results over extended time periods.

For the first time, those seeking better methods for making decisions can follow a plan that will assure a new PROCESS remains intact within the mind. Thought process will improve.

No one can fail who tries.

However, producing the desired result does take practice. If I instructed you to fire an arrow into a bull's eye, it would take time to get it right. You could learn the feel of the drawstring. The balance of the arrow shaft. The sight line and eye placement techniques to master the principal...the aerodynamics of the flight of the arrow. After a good deal of effort your eye would become the practiced eye of the master archer. Your patterns would become successful patterns in the center of the bull's eye.

If you failed to practice your skill for several years, even after winning a shelf of golden trophies, you would no longer hit the same pattern. Oh, you would KNOW how to do it. The skill would never leave you. The knowledge of HOW would never leave you.

However, you would no longer have a practiced eye. Your muscles would no longer respond in the highly organized manner of the practiced archer. With more practice the results would improve and you would, once again, have successful patterns in the center of the bull's eye. You can retrain yourself back to peak performance. Why should the muscle of the mind that sources such behavior be any more unique in process in its highest form of action? THOUGHT.

Now consider; how important is the arrow of the ideas fired from your mind into the future, your reality? How tight do you desire the pattern of future performance to become in the success center of your bull's eye for reality?

YOU CREATE YOUR OWN REALITY.
TO THINK IS TO CREATE.

Your mind IS a muscle. Without regular exercise your mind will perform automatically and unconsciously (without thought). You can wake your mind up. You can keep your mind far more awake than it would be without your perception that THIS priority has merit.

Carl Saegan says in his anthology study about human thought and apes (*Shadows of Forgotten Ancestors*):

"I am now convinced we are 92% like apes. Apes have humor and tell jokes. They play tricks on one another, have social order, self awareness, make tools, discover new things, and protect one another. The only difference between an ape society and our own is the slightest, the tiniest, the smallest degree of intelligence, between mankind and a baboon. However, it is this flicker of degree, and only this, whose consequence is the entire civilization of the world in which we live."

The value of a tiny degree of greater wakefulness in the decision process is the difference of life from cradle to grave as a reactive life in bondage, or a pro-active life in liberation, the life of the SUPER ACHIEVER.

May you be free.............

SUCCESS IS ONE IDEA WEALTH IS THE IDEA RECOGNIZED

Financial success is developed from one idea. Most of the wealthy individuals I know have more than one source of income. The wealthy, successful Super Achievers are consummate networkers. They are sharing their talents and exploiting opportunities.

Typically, they have developed several sources of income. The income sources pay them each month. The technique is known as MULTIPLE INCOME TECHNOLOGIES. They may have many Multiple Income Technologies working for them at the same time.

Multiple Income is not a J.O.B. The idea is not to double or triple your annual income by developing either "another" J.O.B. or even a better J.O.B. Rather, the goal is to double and triple your personal cash flow by developing numerous sources of income. Have you tried to increase your income by moving from J.O.B. to J.O.B. seeking to always get a "better J.O.B."? Did it work? How was your lifestyle?

How can you do what ALL *Super Achievers* have mastered?

First, let's understand and agree that wealthy people contrary to popular rumor live pretty OK lives. They are members of the local country club...usually the BEST country club. They go to the right parties.

They spend lots of time on the golf course. They take long cruise vacations.

Wealthy men and women live the good life. There are more people entering the wealthy group of people during our lifetime than in the history of mankind. There simply is MORE wealth. In 1973 there were around 4100 individuals earning over ONE MILLION DOLLARS a year in the United States. By the year 1993, some twenty years later, the number had risen to over 64,000. Yep. Over 64,000 now earn over ONE MILLION DOLLARS each year. And remember, I am not reporting on net worth or the number of people worth one million dollars. Rather, I am reporting on the skyrocketing group of new Americans that are EARNING over ONE MILLION dollars of personal income each and every year. The American dream is very much alive for those with the vision and vitality to reach out and seize it. For those who already hold it in their hands, share it. Inspire others and use your success to teach and instruct. And always, reach for more.......

So where does wealth come from? What is the source of all wealth? The answer is:

WEALTH COMES FROM ONE SOURCE....UNIQUE AND VALUABLE SERVICES BENEFITING OTHERS.....EXPRESSED IN THE ORIGINAL FORM AS AN IDEA.

Every source of income imaginable can be restated in the terms of this definition for wealth. As long as the service is benefiting others, the wealth will remain. When the service that once benefited is replaced by a better service (idea) the wealth will wither.

From the idea of a HOT PIZZA home delivery (billionaire by the age of forty) to the idea of MS-DOS on a computer (billionaire by the age of thirty) the concept is vivid for all to admire. If putting horse shoes on horses is no longer as valuable to others, the wealth withers. If the typewriter is no longer as valuable as the computer, the new idea takes over in the area of wealth.

The service may be performed by others. Your idea does not necessarily require you. The idea is valuable. The manner in which ACTION is highly organized to apply the idea in form and substance DELIVERS the idea to others. Wealth is the idea itself. Success is the DELIVERY SYSTEM.

A WOW IDEA

Most people stop moving into Success for the following reasons:

1. Old mental conditioning. They don't visualize the service that will create the wealth.
2. Circle of Mediocrity Support Teams: They suppress the dreamer's dream and ground positive energy, neutralizing creative reality.
3. Automated Underachiever Decision-making: Lack of Process Technology for elevating the decision process.

The first rule of success is to overrule old conditioning NOW. The best time to improve a human life IS always the very first time the idea comes to mind! Never put the opportunity off. Never delay.

The next rule is to invest in obtaining skill to develop PROCESS TECHNOLOGY. Elevate the awareness of decision process in your life. For most individuals this will mean investing to attend a class that instructs students on Process Technology.

Finally, learn how to develop CIRCLES of like-minded, nurturing, positive, uplifting team members, who have expressed agreement with your stated PURPOSE (dream).

The only missing element, when these three "turn arounds" are achieved, is the WOW idea to attract the wealth you deserve into your life. Remember you ARE entitled, fully worthy and wholly deserving to receive the wealth you imagine. Exchange a service to receive the wealth.

Action is required. Old style considerations that never lead to action are a waste of time. Time is your most precious item. Wealthy people don't waste much of a twenty-four-hour day. Those who are not wealthy waste much of their time. The possibilities, the services, the benefits humanity would enjoy from the "wake up call" to millions and millions of sleepy decision makers are sufficient to alter the social fabric of evolution.

Most of us fail because we try a go-it-alone approach. Also, we fail to realize the source and power that makes new reality possible:

a) The source of infinite intelligence to which we are all connected.
b) The source of elevated decision-making process to manage our flow of ideas and choices.
c) The source of the selected WOW idea to apply as service to humanity.

Once we visualize that these principals hold the lock on wealth creation, we can begin to succeed!

However, we are still likely to fail on a go-it-alone basis. We need people. As human beings we really do function better together, you know?

By developing a foundation PROCESS to maintain ONGO-ING support for your future success, your chances of winning multiply a thousand fold. Your new team will carry you forward so the principles of success provided for in the pages of the most important success training in the world, will become habitual. You talk about these principles; you think about these principles; you remain highly aware these principles ARE the success. You are less confused by the manifestation of success (the disguise) and you recognize the unfolding, never-ending power within success (the source) contained in the principles listed. This awareness replenishes your success as a never-ending, renewable resource.

Now you are ready to begin selecting your WOW idea. Principles of a WOW Idea include:

1. The idea does not have to be your own. You may recognize a good idea shared by another.
2. You do not need money to ACT on the idea. You need to master how to attract others who have the right resources (your golden circle) who will ACT WITH YOU on the benefits the idea promises to others.
3. You do not need to have specialized knowledge to apply the idea; you only need to master attracting others who have specialized knowledge. Attract your golden circle that will share like-minded enthusiasm for the value the WOW idea promises for the lives of others.

You must truly love the idea. You must feel a sense of WOW inside yourself each time the idea triggers in your mind. You must smile a lot over the WOW idea. You should be able to say the word WOW with conviction and emotion. Your golden circle must all express belief in your idea. Your golden circle must confirm the idea is a WOW for them as well. This recognition is a support system that empowers you to COMPLETE the implementation of the idea into a working reality.

Without emotion for your idea nothing happens. Nothing!

Emotional involvement by you, and from your circle, into the WOW idea is essential for success. You must, like a mental DNA code, place your intelligence, your actions, and your emotional commitment into a helix that forms the entwinement pattern empowering your future success. You must select an idea you can believe in, one that is important to you. The idea must be a PASSION.

Life is full and rich when this passion is present. Life is empty and meaningless when this passion is missing. The degree with which you express yourself with a passionate connection is the degree with which you experience JOY in your life.

We call your idea for new Multiple Income a WOW for a reason. To the extent you have more passion for some idea in life, life is more meaningful. To the extent you have less passion, the living experience is typically more meaningless.

Living life so that you can say each morning "WOW! I love being able to work on this again today...."

Or at night on the pillow self-talking "I am sad this day is over and I can't wait to start again tomorrow, thank you so much for letting me work on THIS WOW, I just love having the opportunity in my life."

Who can live a WOW way of life?

Answer: everyone.

Again...who CAN experience a WOW way of Living LIFE?

Answer again: everyone! You. Everyone you know. No exceptions.

What is stopping you then?

First, the knowledge. Everyone needs to learn some new basic rules to begin.

Second, fear. Fear of many things keeps you from trying or even starting. With so much to gain, you only have one choice really; will you live your life controlled by fears, or in a state of adventure and anticipation?

Third, habit. The old sleepy mind is in the habit of considering as a process. Considering is a sleepy process that is not decision-making expressed in action. There is no choice, just a process of review and filing. Nothing ever happens. You and you alone can break this old mind habit of establishing mental importance.

How?

Pick your team and form your first Golden CIRCLE. Let nothing stop you.

First project, work on developing a WOW. Spend one, two or three Golden Circle Mastermind Team meetings until you get IT. The entire process won't take three weeks and may be only days away from reading this sentence.

How big will your resulting life change become from this almost too-easy exercise?

Try it and you tell me.

I'm smiling now because I already KNOW the answer?

NETWORKING
SKILL OF THE CENTURY

Networking is a skill which, once mastered, will accelerate success like no other skill. Networking can be used in any field of endeavor to accelerate success. For the purpose of SNAP, the focus of attention for network activity will be limited to the development of income.

NETWORKING IS A PROCESS OF HIGHLY-ORGANIZED ACTIVITY THAT ACCELERATES RESULTS.

Results accelerate for every team by the work of connecting to the right expert with the right contact, the right information, the right access to capital or data, that can deliver the consequence desired. Once the objective is clearly stated, the next mission is to **take action** that will accelerate obtaining the objective.

For far too many of us, objective fulfillment is a matter of planning not action. Months, quarters, years are spent in only the planning stage.

Life should be spent. More important than capital you invest, Life should be fully spent in service...**spent** in highly organized patterns of taking action. Life should NEVER be spent in waste through largely unproductive considering instead of deciding.

Decisions are always expressed in action.

Highly organized thinking always expresses itself in the form of action that is highly organized.

To obtain a goal, one must first state the goal in clear terms. The terms should be something your entire SUCCESS TEAM can agree upon. Consensus is required.

A written statement of AGREEMENT is required. A breakthrough takes place when your circle quickly comes into agreement to support a single, well-stated purpose for the effort under development.

Far too little has been written about consensus. When a success team is out of consensus, someone on the team is less supportive. Majority rule won't cut it.

Those who are the minority are working to "be right" in some area of decision. At some level these individuals are undermining success. They secretly "hope" the opportunity to say "I told you so" or "If you had only listened to me" will emerge.

Consensus means 100% unanimous support. Consensus is not required on all subjects. Consensus is required in the areas of:

- Team Agreement for the definition of all missions.
- Team Agreement for all primary team actions.
- Team Agreement for priority setting.

Consensus is not required in the area of source. The team leader may as the "source" of the idea, edit direction and call for a specific policy or course change that becomes the new PROCESS for making up new agendas, new missions, etc. The team is required to provide POSITIVE LIKE-MINDED SUPPORT for the team leader. If team members cannot provide individual support because they find they are NOT like-minded (on numerous subjects as opposed to one subject) the individual member should leave the team, without impact on the remaining team members.

No one on the team may provide input that is negative, grounding, or less than uplifting.

Evidence of like-minded support is nurturing, complimenting, and uplifting input expressed on a repetitive basis. All success teams strive to perfect this discipline of SNAPPING OUT of the negative circles we live within to positive circles we seek to live within.

Once the team has agreed unanimously to support the mission for the Network Team session, the Networking begins. Networking seeks to involve team members in a commitment. Note that all team members are lifted up by the new positive environment they find themselves performing within. As this new positive environment is experienced repetitively, team members develop judgment to SWITCH negative old-mind inventory off and leave the conditioned common world mind at the office or home. The elevated, positive, new world mind every one of us is striving to create in our lives, and in the lives of those we love, is turned on and kept on longer.

Networking is both an internal and an external commitment.

Team Members engage in immediate effort to identify worthy introductions they know, or from people they know can MAKE a key resource introduction. The introduction should be powerful, immediate, and able to act on the written mission statement adopted by the team. The idea is to introduce the right men and women in the best position to achieve the mission. The goal is to obtain the objective in the shortest time period. Guides for Networking include the following structural rules:

1. Mastermind Creative Team sessions should be opened and closed on separate days from Networking Sessions.
2. Network Team Members are selected for skill useful to the project and suggested by your Mastermind Team. Your Network Team may contain one or many different members from Your Mastermind Team.
3. The meeting opens with a ten minute editorial session to obtain unanimous agreement on the written mission for which the specific session seeks to accelerate achievement.
4. The formal Network activity begins when the team leader uses the word GO to open the session.
5. Members of the Network Success Team use telephones and interactive discussion to trigger access to key persons who will complete the mission. Meetings are set up on the spot. Delegation of who meets with whom is decided upon as the meeting schedule fills.
6. Network sessions are closed when the team leader calls for the meeting to be formally closed (90 Minutes maximum per session). Use the phrase END or COMPLETE.
7. The energy of the session is completed with a blessing, if the Team is so disposed.

Elevated awareness in the decision PROCESS is best maintained for short, power-burst sessions. Maximum creative process is derived from concentrating awareness (as with a condenser for a power coil) into a tight loop or circle, over a short term of build up and then release the energy.

A large desktop calendar is used to track meeting follow-through appointments. The confirmed SNAP follow-through appointments are listed in the calendar, using a red (for red hot) marker pen. These meetings are always recorded into a large desk calendar CONTROL system, representing actual meeting dates and times developed from each High Performance Team SNAP networking session. Confirm appointments you have completed in follow through as you process the SEE ME cards from each SNAP session. Who sourced the lead and appointment is recorded. Who is fulfilling each meeting via fixed delegation of duties is also recorded. Computer schedule management comes later, if at all.

TIP: your super conscious mind "thinks" in color.

The pending (yet to be confirmed) meetings are listed using a blue market pen.

The large calendar is a visual to the team leader for each mission purpose. The team leader uses the calendar as a SUBCONSCIOUS MIND STIMULATOR. A stimulator that triggers:

- Team Members to see who IS and who IS NOT contributing connections at each SNAP session.
- Overall Success for all participating teams.
- One success leads to another, recording referral from prime leads to even more precise prime leads!

Keep successes out front where everyone can see them. Color mapping is useful. The mind responds to color in magical ways. Use colors liberally in planning all your sessions.

Everyone can upgrade High Performance team completion flow by elevating the process of meetings. High Performance teams should meet for task and completion. Task meetings are short. Execution is the foremost purpose of each session. Leaders set the pace and tone of each meeting. Meetings create solution delegations and follow up against fixed time lines. High Performance team meetings lead to high performance results you can count on.

Expert coaches can assist in improving process. Reframe priorities often. As you complete one priority set move on to the next. Stay ahead of your own timeline. Apply the high performance formats modified to your own comfort process to accelerate results. Every CEO can and should improve the results they realize today. If your system remains unchanged, your results will remain the same.

Today, alumni from leading Biz-to-Biz CEO Retreats, like the famous Harold Allen Brokerage "by-invitation-only" annual investor previews in Idaho, create superior networks and value to major University graduate contacts. Attending the in-crowd, short-lists of IBI Global, CEO-to-CEO and related week-long retreats, explodes network base for senior management of any size business.

Positioning – you were born to choose. Only "you" can reposition yourself. Only you can reposition, repackage, rebrand and reprice your future values to the Global Village market. Both you and your organization create new income as a result of the following ingredients:

• Improved planning (which can begin now)

- Elevated team talent
- Resources (networks) to execute on the former two

No matter how rich your existing network – you were born to choose expanded quality and quantity for what comes next. Global Village networking is the skill of the century. New century CEO-to-CEO retreats are the mechanism to define mental software upgrades – as well as open platforms to elevate your existing network. Plan to invest time and resources to attend network expanding capacity via one or more executive-level retreats annually.

The network exchange will be larger than your own. As you acquire elevated network throughput capacity, you add to the network of others, dramatically leveraging your own functionality to the Global Village. Cooperation organizing principles increase the velocity, acceleration and momentum of network value.

EXPANDED NETWORKS WARP DRIVE PERFORMANCE

It is now possible to dramatically replace decades of time to establish relationship networks using modern age communication protocols. As you grow and maintain higher quality networks, your entire team improves output.

TEAM WORK MAKES THE DREAM WORK

*NETWORKS EXPONENTIALLY INCREASE
POWER TO PERFORM*

SWITCH OF THE MIND

Networking is an exercise for the mind. One unique feature of Networking, as defined in this book, is that Networking creates whole brain involvement via accelerated creative process. Features of committing that YOU will take action and network on a regular basis include:

- Whole brain involvement (left/right brain commitment)
- Access to the subconscious mind
- Improved state of creativity
- Improved decision-making (long-lasting effects)
- Measurable real life results in less time
- Speed: improved group performance via making more decisions of higher quality

We have discovered that CEOs can acquire a Super Achiever mindset and remain in Prime at peak performance at all times. Better mental software is required and upgrades with better code continue to flood the market. Loading this software on your personal server is the key to opening the better code locked inside you.

By working through countless experiments we have discovered that a magic MIND SWITCH does exist. This Switch will work for everyone, without exception. Let go of any fear that the process will not work for you, because it will.

However, certain ingredients are required before the MIND SWITCH will work. For example, a power switch will not work unless there is power. There must be wire to transmit the power. The Switch completes the circuit that allows the light to light, the motor to roar, the disposal to dispose.

A human being requires certain ingredients to upgrade mental software, not dissimilar to the switch on your wall at home. First, you must have power. Power is supplied by a TEAM of like-minded individuals – the battery pack for the mind is your support team. You choose the quality of your team support by the quality you choose to **give** in team support.

Something happens inside each one of us when we take a seat beside a TEAM we know will support us with loving, nurturing, unconditional trust and encouragement. Most of us don't expect such support. Most of us have forgotten that it is we, each of us, who CHOOSE to create or to deny this form of support in our lives. We can achieve this level of support if we desire it.

A key to the improved software for the mind everyone seeks is to accept the notion that we acquire the battery pack of unconditional support from our teams when we GIVE such support to others – without compromise -

A human being also requires the wire to transmit the power. The wire in this case is the Team's agreement (commitment) to faithfully invest time and effort into the project you have created. Team intention sets the pace of transmission for the product of unconditional support (better decisions = more completions) down the wire to the end user. The end user is the defined customer for the team work being done at the moment. Without 100% team agreement (intention) the attention becomes divided and the juice flowing down the wire is fragmented. Taking the short time allocations required to ask for and to obtain core agreement from High Performance Teams is a leadership role.

Finally, you must have a PURPOSE (your priority of today) to throw your switch on and off, which is why you called the meeting into session in the first place. Careful priority management defines the underlying decision work of the mind – selecting "this is more important than that" as a demarcation in how one group uses its TIME versus how another group uses its time. The largest cost to business is the misuse of time through the misallocation of priority sets. Leadership becomes masterful when leadership habitually redefines the priority sequence for any narrow, near-term performance mission.

Improved Priority Management IS the Mission.

How often should you schedule a session of this nature? Napoleon Hill says in his famous book, THINK AND GROW RICH, that anyone committed to access Peak Performance decision-making, should create HIGH PERFORMANCE team meetings (he refers to as a mastermind) once each week. Today, with easier conferencing ability and modern communications, such an idea is even more convenient. Napoleon Hill recognized these team meetings as the best exercise for the muscle of the mind.

Remember: Success IS a Learned Behavior. Everyone can learn to elevate his or her mental software for greater success regardless of the prior success attained. The key CEO quality to upgrade mental software is your desire to begin.

Knowing more about how your mind makes decisions opens the pathway to knowing more about your personal decision process. Group High Performance Teamwork tends to reframe the priority setting process – anchor better code inside the mind – as new habits are embraced as a better way.

The mind always embraces a better way.

*Who throws the switch he or she can't see
or locate in the dark of night?*

WHAT YOU CAN'T VISUALIZE ISN'T REAL FOR YOU .....

I'M BLIND,
DEAF AND DUMB

Do you find far too many on your team act as if they are blind, deaf and dumb? If you really look at the way those with untrained mental software live their lives, many untrained human CPUs simply give off signals that tell others, "Hey, I'm not capable of achieving greater success in my life" or "I'm happy living my life in resignation which precludes my taking risks to win more, do more, be more in my own life." We each operate super sensitive radio receivers that automatically pick up such signals and process them. We recognize infinite numbers of non verbal cues as to the programs of others – which activate without our having to do anything – every single time we pass near another spiritual being in our lives. We communicate by high bandwidth, wireless signals each of us well knows how to read instantly – because the core program for this function is built into our MOTHERBOARDS. Unfortunately, security being what it is these days, virus written programs pass effortlessly along and become attached to our own base operating system. The virus code becomes "real" for us. In fact, we will defend our old models for lower performance as if our (programming) life is depending upon it. Amazingly, we don't even know why our emotions are so linked to older, far less effective code.

It takes a highly retrained CPU to embrace new mental software upgrades as if they came from the source of all programming, which, of course, is reality.

When provided with new possibility, virus programs define us. Some of the markers of a virus program operating on a CEO's mental CPU include:

> "This or that new idea just won't work for me" (old conditioning kicking in).

> "I know I could never realize this new concept or integrate it into my present output." (Hogwash-it's what you really want anyway!)

> "No one will meet with me and be on my golden circle if I do this or that." (Yes, they will. Old code follows strong leadership – ask and you SHALL receive – Golden Circle Team Underwriting for new performance gains.)

Self-talk is destructive when shifted to "why we can't" discussions inside your private mental conversations. Running much like invisible DVDs of the mind these old programs run very powerfully all day. Learning to pay attention to what these "old tapes" are playing is a Super Achiever mindset known as self perception. Becoming keenly aware of your mental DVD thought inventory becomes a major departure point for the freedom to play new DVD programming – improved movies of the mind – for your mental CPU. Defeating negative self-talk, the great illusionist, is often perceived as a risk reducer versus a success killer (which, in fact, such DVD tapes truly are).

CEOs invest countless hours lacking acute self perception, playing endless movies of the mind, in time-wasting debates of "why action can't or shouldn't be taken" to proactively impact future reality. Such mental DVDs represent tapes of non reality.

Such DVD programs are pure fiction. The conversation creating reality but rather preserving the status quo is a condition of mind epidemic in society known as self delusion or reactive thinking. Fear appears when improvement (pro-active thinking), mislabeled as change, is translated by the mind program into emotional fear. The viruses of the mind fear all change as a possible virus graveyard. Protection built into virus programs enlarges fear to protect the virus from a condition known as deletion.

All improvement is typically mistranslated to represent change by virus programs. Super Achievers experience new thought and new action as a welcomed opportunity. Fear is replaced by virus-free CPUs as an emotion of excitement and anticipation. Fear is a "marker" for virus thinking.

TIP: Reprogram any idea of change (via self talk suggestion) into improvement to lower the fear threshold mislabeling creates in your emotion when progress is the desired destination. Dispel fear. Take charge of your mental conversations. Be alert to the mental conversations taking place inside your CPU via self perception. How important are the audit habits for the thinking stream of your mind? If your computer is unregulated by superior applications (of mind), your flow of data may appear like gibberish on the screen of your mind. Discover:

"I don't need this or that new result."

"I'm already happy and successful I can't see where a new plateau would help me."

"I'm struggling just to keep up. I can't possibly meet once a week with yet another thing to work on."

"I'm enjoying my CEO-at-the-top prestige, I don't want to expand service any further to the Global Village!"

"I've earned my retirement – why should I consider any more contribution anyway?"

All mind junk to any Super ACHIEVER THINKER, all self-talk fighting for control of the way it was yesterday – defeats the adventure, thrill and full blast potential of living life most completely in contribution. Contribution is the one human cash flow wherein plenty is never enough.

Illusion is forever trying to sit you down inside the circle of mediocrity instead of in the middle of your new circle, your new GOLDEN CIRCLE of expanded power and abundance derived as a consequence of expanded Global Village Contribution. New contribution to society is the correct, programmatic way of living life as a spirit being human. You were born a Super Achiever.

RESIGNATION IS A LEARNED BEHAVIOR

The choice to contribute more is always a right decision. The lack of greater contribution is later regretted by the mind and instantly regretted by the spirit.

Just say NO to thoughts that bind you to the comforts of status quo. You won't grow in the future of the status quo and the status quo won't grow you.

Learn to smile at thoughts that lead to a lack of personal growth or a limit of Global Village Contribution. There is no glass ceiling on a Super Achiever's contribution. There is no natural cap to the spirit's creative output.

Status quo retro thoughts will come to all of us from time to time. Everyone has thoughts that slow the potential of the Super Achiever mental software - accented whenever you approach new adventures in the human living safari. Make a decision to always move forward, out into the bush of excellence, and away from the open plains of mediocrity. Lions, tigers and bears await their evening meal on the open fields of mediocrity.

Take your camera and find a wild new animal you have

never captured (a new idea to contribute to the Global Village) and place each one into the photo album of your life. Winning grows you – as you grow winning. Winning grows everyone you share life beside. Winning is fertilizer for the soul. And you deserve bigger WINS every month of your life. No one reaches a destination when human potential is the finish line. There never was, nor can there ever be, a finish line for human potential. Imagine if Michelangelo had ceased to paint because he had "enough"; or if Beethoven had never created the Fifth Symphony; or Bill Gates hadn't followed through to create upgrades for Windows because he had enough; or the Dali Llama elected to "retire" because he was complete with his lifetime contributions to the Global Village.

As a Super Achiever, your best contribution to society is always your next book – your next division or new product introduction – your next clinic or office expansion – your next brochure, your next advertisement – your next board position – your next mentorship to a developing company and their CEO - your next service to the rest of us.

TIP: most great thinkers don't see themselves as giving great services back to the rest of us. Why? Because of mindless education and prior conditioning. Virus ridden DVD films playing inside the mind limit human output in all organized endeavors more than any other environment or aspect of the human experience. As a candle is replaced with electric light – education, an instant solution, is attained.

Consider cancer. Cancer is a dis-ease that is a reaction of cells to genetic predisposition – error in code replication – or toxicity introduced in the human system. Genetic repair kits will absolutely eliminate the pain and dis-comfort – dis-function and dis-ease that human spirits experience in a condition known as cancer. Cancer is bad code. Code repair deletes the cancer virus from the system. The total and absolute removal of cancer is a condition of EDUCATION and KNOWELDGE. Human kind spends more of its capital on prison systems, by a factor of sixty to one, than it invests in cancer research (code repair and virus deletion). Humanity will soon have the knowledge. As with blowing out a candle and turning on the light switch, the truth of better code will set us free. Mankind invests more in prisons that it does in space research and exploration, when space holds the keys to the knowledge to remove dis-ease from the planet while we open windows of new knowledge to the stars. Examine the difference of transportation as one idea, where in a single generation we moved from saddling the horse and ox, to throwing a switch to launch a shuttle into orbit. Human knowledge is an idea we do not retire from gaining or giving.

Retirement is a virus and requires deletion.
SUPER ACHIEVERS NEVER RETIRE

Untrained team formation results in virus thinkers retarding team performance. Educated team selection results in virus-free thinkers propelling team performance to higher output efficiencies. The difference between the two modes of team selection is a difference between Super Achiever mindsets and non Super Achiever mindsets. Team selection is a learned behavior.

Most of the journey through life performance is invested beside teams we created with little thought or preparation. We didn't put in the training and thought to carefully develop High Performance teams as a topic of mind.

Team creation is a topic of mind.....

Our personal and organizational output is largely defined by the mental programs we upgrade to our computer of mind; the coaches we employ to help us upgrade mental software; and the teams we choose to assist us in maintaining optimal software performance over time. Our desire to be accepted, to be loved, is so great that we permit weak teams to surround us, compromising into mediocrity in exchange for the penalty free lifestyle of leaderless sailing. It takes strength to place your hand on the tiller of your future. Destiny is not an easy sail. The soul is always paid in the currency of its request. If the mind requests payment in worship and applause – you will receive worship and applause. If your mind requests payment in elevated knowledge and performance you'll receive payment in elevated performance and knowledge. Your mind will always make you right.

TIP: Be self observant to your requests of mind because you are always receiving precisely what you are asking for. You may not know it, but to alter output you must alter input.

A weak team is any team that will hold back your Super Achiever mindset. A weak team is any team or team member who will depreciate your mental performance. If your self esteem is compromised in any way – your team is weak. Your team is strong if your performance is in overflow and so are you. Overflow is the state of the High Performance Super Achiever team mindset.

Nothing is more important than your imagination to the human experience! Your imagination is your ability to create new benefits each of us can share. Your imagination is the HOW you are made in the image and likeness of God. Your Imagination is what inspires human beings to achieve destiny outside recorded human experience. Your imagination is the savings account for the Lord's Holy Capital – inspirations. Where else could the divine plan deposit its most sacred commodity (inspired ideas) save into the depository of your mind? Your virus-cleansed CPU becomes fertile ground for these new ideas. Your imagination is the heart that pumps blood into the Global Village for all the rest of us. When all of us contribute maximally such that "no spirit is left behind," we have achieved the healthy blood pressure the cooperative Global Village requires to explore the universe.

There is only one potential – unlimited......

Within each one of us is a universe of untapped potential. Unlocking this potential is far easier if you maintain a fully open mind to the idea such potential is the most important priority for humanity. Assess the collective movement of the cooperative Global Village away from competition virus thinking – with a simple yard stick. Monitor social output to invest more into public education by large ratios than we invest into prison construction and upkeep. Equate fear removal from society and a victory on fighting crime as a condition of tearing prisons down versus building new ones. Adopt a belief that the pendulum also swings back – as new laws remove hundreds of criminalized codes – to "roll back freedom" everywhere in the Global Village as cooperation dispels fear and terror from the human condition. Right thinking is the process and "perfection" is the consequence.

Super Achievers have discovered a few basic rules about success.

The first rule is the MASTER RULE of Success which works like this:

REALITY CHECK: You and only you create your reality. No one else creates your reality for you. No Circumstance, individual or group is responsible for the reality you experience right now or tomorrow. No spouse. No supervisor. No family member. No lover. No friend. No religious adviser. No one. Only you created your reality. Only you can change your reality. You can do anything, be anything, live anywhere, own anything and create anything you desire in the global village - all in less time than you imagine. All the struggles you have ever known are lessons you commanded into your own life - and each is wonderful. Your reality prepares you as you prepare your reality.

The second rule of success is equally important and should be studied until accepted:

CAUSE AND EFFECT: Your results are a consequence of your process for making choice. Many factors (conditioning) make up your personal process for making decisions. Until a CEO leader changes his/her process (system) for making a decision, output results will remain unchanged. Our results are frozen decisions. Old habits - without help and coaching - remain invisible to us and control our life output without our awareness (reactive mindsets). If you improve the mechanism for making decisions, you will forever improve your results. Super Achiever Mindsets are proactive builders of their future. Non Super Achievers have yet to attain mind skills to improve their process for making better decisions.

How do you improve your process for making a decision? This question is the fundamental one affecting long term life improvement and the Super Achiever mindset. The answer is not a simple one. First, you must be willing to examine the way you make a decision at any point in time. The examination must become a habitual behavior. Typically, an individual requires an expert coach to advise and assist with the self-review process. For the CEO, an in-industry coach is desirable with decision reformation technology masters desired. You must ALWAYS be self examining as to WHY you selected a particular action or output and the degree of intervention, or lack of same, applied to individual decisions. To the extent possible you might also develop a mental scale that, in time, becomes a natural process – to determine if any future course of action (decision) is more or is less – cooperative versus competitive.

Attempt to quickly replace competitive choices – with cooperative output – an exercise which of itself helps to reform decision quality. As you take time (expressed in nano seconds of mental processing to the stream of thoughts flowing through the mind in any minute) to "reflect, judge and quality control" your output decisions, you elevate your personal process for making improved choices.

Quite naturally – by training the mind to copy what it determines is a better way "for process" in resolution to any challenge or priority (thinking) – always selecting with superior coaches – associating with peer-to-peer networks where CEOs all work on their mental software you speed up the mind software upgrades to decision-reformation self training. Smarter CEOs join retreats on a regular basis to establish peer-to-peer "checks" that by intention represent peer groups who seek to upgrade mental software at the top. There is no substitute for dedicated time to upgrade mental software during the course of a calendar year. All other decisions should be delayed for mental upgrades to the system of making choice – to improve – and then process the pending priority grid to solution. As with any skill, practice makes perfect. Repetition is required. Audit standards that are comfortable for your personality and temperament must be designed. No single system fits everyone. We are all highly deferential learners and mind skills training requires trust, confidence, and some surrender by the individual to "appointed" teachers. Employee reward programs that involve superior mind skill training for team manufacture decision-reformation improvement to the mental software for groups. Invest in them. No other organizational investment produces equal measure of output gains. To the extent that measurable standards to move organization systems toward a cooperative versus a competitive model are employed – output results improve rapidly.

I once had a student who was laboring over coming to one of my classes on Peak Performance Team Training. The student owned a small, profit-making business in Phoenix. During a speaking tour, I met with the student, and he explained his business to me and how he dreamed of making his business grow in the near term to a multi-state, multi-million dollar operation. I gave the student some new directional ideas (inspirations) that carried his dream (plan) to the destination he envisioned in one giant step. The student became very excited as he saw the completion more clearly and as the financial reality unfolded with greater detail. His plan experienced the Velocity, Acceleration and Momentum of improved decision making – to drive new results into his life.

The student next told me he would attend one of our CEO-to-CEO retreat programs, but not for six months. He was going to miss the next IBI Global Retreat (one weekend away) because he had made another plan for that week. Under normal circumstances, I would have accepted the student's explanation and thought nothing more of it. I was busy with many more CEOs huddled around the podium where my lecture had just adjourned.

From long experience, I knew BETTER and I could see the

time the CEO could never reclaim spinning away from him. I stopped the student cold, even while others were waiting to meet with me. I said to the young man:

"I want to KNOW exactly what decision created a plan that is a higher priority than the CEO retraining opportunity coming up – so that I can study your process for making better choices. I believe next week will forever alter your decision-making process and dramatically improve your organization's income. Tell me what plan keeps you from improving your entire framework for making decisions as well as your output results rising?"

I explained how, in my view, the student had shown a history of making poor decisions. Wrong choices in business. Decisions to "consider" his opportunities now and again but never acting on the opportunities. All the time, he was avoiding taking action that would deliver the results he was seeking. I explained what a success killer "consideration versus decision making" was to the use of time – the critical space asset.

I asked the student why he COULD not, why he WOULD not be at the CEO retreat in the coming week.

Finally, I discovered that the reason was a fishing trip he had planned with some friends. He was going to delay, for a long while, his near term success and the choice of obtaining the tools to reform his entire business, life and future – to go fishing. While going fishing IS important, of course - it is easily rescheduled if the mind elects to make a reset choice. Super Achievers reframe their priority choices by the hour – non super achievers lack skill to manage priority options.

I informed the student that opportunity – the best and most important opportunities in life - almost always arrive at a critical space decision point in time - that critical space which challenges you. Super Achievers become sensitive to habitually resetting and rescheduling to make sure they do not miss the FAN-

TASTIC opportunities that flow into their lives. Typically, opportunity comes at a time that appears to be inopportune because the fishing trips of life are already planned. Super Achiever Mindsets use the critical space to reframe core decisions forever improving the options permitted by TIME.

Opportunity typically conflicts with other things we had PLANNED. Super Achievers make immediate decisions to RECOGNIZE the FANTASTIC opportunities for what THEY truly represent as lakes of vast potential and apply the critical space to improve the old plan (a new decision by itself) to a far higher level of activity – and instantly capture each new opportunity. Divine law always delivers more opportunities to those who grasp them - versus those who avoid them. In this case it was appropriate, even compelling, for the student to be in the training for the coming weekend and to reschedule (if only for a few days) the fishing trip.

I asked the student to go to the back of the now-emptying room and have a seat. I asked him to examine in his own private thoughts of when he had great, even the best opportunities of his life. I asked him to honestly assess if he did not at each point, have to change his plan, and struggle with a decision. I asked him to examine when he got engaged and married, had his first child, birthed his young business and so forth – IF amazing timing challenges didn't whirl around his decisions. The threshold of opportunity can be wide open, but we can be deaf, dumb and blind to see it – while WE focus on the fishing trips of life.

I suggested he was, indeed, facing one of the GREATEST OPPORTUNITIES of his entire lifetime, and why would he postpone such an opportunity even one moment. Wasn't the DECISION worthy of the benefit (upgrading his mental software)?

I instructed the student to decide solely on the aspect if a bead of sweat would form on his brow while he was thinking. I indicated he probably would hear a little voice inside telling him that the right decision was to reschedule the fishing trip, and to act on improving his entire future right now, this weekend, without delay. I told him enrolling was a self-enrollment process – in which only he could enroll himself into a better future as CEO of his own enterprise. No other CEO could enroll him. We could not enroll him. He would have to enroll himself – if ever he would.

If he did not experience consternation earmarked by a tiny bead of sweat, I indicated he should just leave (as he was in the back and no one would even notice) and attend some future class, if he was ever so disposed when he felt it was "easier" to schedule. He walked back to sit as he paused to apply the critical space for Super Achiever mindset decision making.

 Much later this young business owner came up to the front of the room (frankly, I had forgotten and thought he had left) and handed me a completed CEO Retreat enrollment form and the tuition. I was a bit surprised actually.

I was taken aback by the way his face had changed. He had such a struggle about him before. Now he was almost laughing. He held a huge smile and was beaming. He grabbed my hand, and pointed to the enrollment form saying, "That's the mark from the drop of sweat that fell off my nose – (the ink had run a bit on his signature) - "as it became so clear to me," he continued – "the fishing trip can be rescheduled- the right decision was to be in class not catching fish.......I'd catch all the fish the rest of my life and they'd be so much larger."

This young CEO has completed his master plan for a huge business, made the key connections to raise the capital and make the plan really work. He developed a program to enlarge his existing ten-year old company to a nationwide company in only months. Most importantly, he improved his process for making a decision – which is still in play almost a decade later. This CEO has taught a lot of other CEOs about fishing – along the way – a lesson he is well qualified to sweat over. He's become a Super Achiever, an A plus student for the mindset.

He now enjoys a new life supported by several GOLDEN CIRCLES. He is thrilled to receive loving, uplifting support from others, while giving positive like-minded support away whenever the opportunity arises.

What he did by accident in the meeting room, he learned to do on purpose. The consequence is decision skill; advanced mind skill all of us should pay greater attention to; skill in making better choices by being more awake at the moment a decision is made – the critical space.

Critical space is the moment in time when decisions are being born.

Success IS a learned behavior. You are learning a great deal about success right now – as the most successful readers have not yet written their best play, book or symphony. God has big plans for you and your best work lies far into the future – far beyond your sight line – if you open your mind to the idea – the way you make decisions can always substantially improve. Unless you have traveled in a worm hole or absolutely cured cancer you still have so much more to learn.

You may say, but I am really deaf, dumb and blind when it comes to having an IDEA about WHAT steps to take to improve my personal decisions. Grab the critical space and decide to attend a decision reformation retreat for CEO leaders – there are endless quality offerings. Hire a personal decision trainer – seek out the best.

Make the most important critical space decision of the next period of time –Decide to BEGIN all over again – renew yourself.

SHAKING THE FEAR OUT OF LIFE

Fear is an emotion. Fear just comes. Like any feeling. Fear will sometimes simply be a passing energy wave. At other times a fear storm will fill you with anxiety. Fear is a feeling. Fear will always pass through you. By you. Around you. Fear is typically nothing more than a passing fancy. Get used to it. Don't hang onto it. Your emotional excess electricity is simply sorting itself out and restoring juice for later use. Nothing can hurt you. Nothing will hurt you. Fear is an illusion of mind. Not a reality of existence.

The good news is that you can use and apply fear to obtain benefits. Fear is a subject discussed as a primary topic in other sections of your Super Achiever education. It is important now to make a key decision to never make a choice in life when you are **fearful**. Let fear pass through you. When you feel that the fear is no longer gripping you, then make your decision and take action immediately. Never make a choice without **taking action** to position your mental decision into time and space through action. <u>Decisions are incomplete when action is lacking.</u> Decisions without action equal considerations. Millions are impotent in life because they fail to make decisions and take action. They are held hostage by a lifetime of considerations.

Actions lead to success. Considerations lead nowhere. Actions express thinking. Considerations are a waste of time.

Many people find it impossible to take action without first deliberating endlessly on ALL the ramifications. This path leads away from success. Prudent review of the requirements to implement a plan of action is always wise. Conditioned meandering down the path of endless considerations makes for an empty life of inactivity.

VISION

Vision is the key expression of Master Manifestors. Super Achievers are master manifestors. Human organizations require clarity of vision to propel elevated performance. Improved output from any size organization requires vision renewal over frequent points of time. Expressing the common vision every eighteen months on an organization-wide basis is a critical decision for CEO leaders at the top.

For smaller organizations, vision transmission meetings may represent meal meetings every eighteen months. You will reward key employees and teams via recognition. You will inspire with vision renewal. You will ask for 100% support of the reframed vision plan.

For organizations using distance learning systems for larger groups – (www.superteaching.org) – entire families of all employees are invited to group meeting facilities – via designated EPNs or Employee Participation Nights. Key employees are rewarded and recognized – inspiring the entire group globally. Requests for 100% support of the new vision plan are made to employees and their families who via the human response to "inclusion versus exclusion" respond with higher output performance. Nothing rallies employee performance like frequently scheduled EPNs to transmit the common vision from the top down.

Refocusing organizations on common vision is a feature of

Super Achiever organizations operated with cooperation principles "inside." Vision is a shared sequence of pending events that grow the organization's service to benefit the global village. CEO teams are responsible for renewing the vision plan of the past into the vision plan of the future. Boards insure the vision plan is consistent with organizational intent and Global Village ethics.

Ethics represent an inside/out versus an outside/in aspect of the Super Achiever. Non Super Achievers think non ethics. Super Achievers correctly equate all output as improved service to the increasingly more cooperative Global Village. Super Achievers acquire competitive minded organizations or retire them into cooperative transformations. Vision planning is a tool of Cooperation Transformation.

Every organization requires Vision Planning to survive and to prosper. If vision renewal is postponed the organization tends to wither. If vision renewal becomes a priority for cooperative organizational planning – organizational growth tends to speed up.

Vision planning optimally takes place in vision planning retreats. CEOs charged to renew organizational vision lead or host the retreat. A vision planning consultant expert may also be hired to lead the retreat. Vision planning retreats generally last one week for larger organizations and less time for smaller organizations. A team of three to five vision planning Super Achievers with seven being the maximum – are selected by the CEO. Vision planning ideally occurs for every team within an organization – and for the organization as a whole in the Master Vision Planning Renewal retreat. Master Retreats are hosted every eighteen months maximum but twelve months is best.

Changes in Global Village Marketing are taking place so rapidly – as the earth shrinks to smaller, planet-wide service systems – pro active vision planners must adapt to ever-renew-ing conditions. The time to renew older vision plans has moved from thirty-six months to eighteen months. No greater priority exists to the CEO team leader than the renewal of common or-ganizational vision.

- How will your goods and services arrive to the Global Village?
- How will you grow step-by-step your new divi-sions, products or services?
- What resources are planned and markets envi-sioned?
- What new tools will be employed?
- How does your organization look when the new vision is realized?
- How can everyone best support your new vision?

New vision must be created and transmitted to become mani-fest. Without new vision all organizational systems wither and die. The most challenging work output of any organized human activity is the work effort to create and plan new vision. This raw creative work – much like writing a book from scratch– or a new item of music – is both an agony and ecstasy. It was not easy for a Michael Eisner to renew the vision of a Walt Disney into a form of himself and his imagination. Today, the vision of a Walt Disney has transformed itself into the vision of a Michael Eisner to the Global Village – which itself is being transformed by the cooperation principles that one day will move Disney into space and under the seas. Vision renewal is the growth asset upon which all organizations rest as a foundation – true for families – true for nations. Families need common vision renewal. Nations require common vision renewal.

Vision planning is the most exciting organizational endeavor – as the manifestation of the human test first occurs in the critical space of the vision planning decisions. Stages of a Vision Planning Retreat follow general principles that include:

1. Arrival – rules or engagement and social
2. Review – restatement of the prior vision – assessment
3. Challenge – review of the issues facing the future
4. Creation – integration planning for renewed vision master plan
5. Resolution – time lines and delegation of the created vision plan

The vision team should be comprised of Super Achievers with the mindset and skill to co-create the renewed vision. Teammates should be liked minded and of unconditional support to the team leader and process. Generally, the rule for such teams:

- Three and you're free (you have a core team)
- Five and you thrive (you have a mindset)
- Seven and you're in heaven (you're complete in efficiency)
- Anything more and you're a committee (begins to retard results vs. contribute to them)

Professional consultants are on call in a video phone world – as CEOs maintain each vision plan retreat to remain on purpose. Paid Vision Plan Retreat Professionals for any size organization are available to prep such meetings or control the entire process. Vision plans should become virtually locked to avoid refocus during the planning interval. During the eighteen months new inspirations benefiting the organization are placed into a Vision Planning agenda box – to be included or discarded by the CEO Vision planners in the week of prep prior to each event.

The most important part of frequent and repetitive vision renewal in the cooperation organization is a value known as transmission. Vision plans that are unclear create divided results. Vision plans that are "clear and compelling" create Velocity Acceleration and Momentum – VAM. Transmission of vision plans is the VAM for completion of vision plan retreats.

Teams affected by the vision plan must be included versus excluded to develop VAM. A large organization employee night looks like – VIP invited guests and families attend Employee Participation Nights at host hotels – via three screen distance learning technology – whereby music is playing upon arrival to institutional theme images.

At the start all locations "light up" as a major organizational "show" depicts themes of the old and new image flowing into the future.

Senior VIPs next appear on screens to reward and recognize team leaders – who appear by camera to the entire audience nationally or even worldwide –

The CEO is introduced and appears on all three screens to recognize some of the VIP leaders and vision plan teammates.

The CEO transmits the entire vision plan and asks for family and employee 100% support.

The CEO finally introduces the FUTURE OF THE ORGANIZATION – and a finale (the best) DVD is presented that features the vision plan fully executed – the future.

Employees leave with the organizations theme music and images – taking the EPN with them as the organization is renewed from the family support team to the core team – system wide.

Typically EPNs are held after hours – and are optional to attend. Data base records of who fails to attend can be maintained as indicators of like minded support – or the lack of support – sought in any organization. EPNs become barometers for these measurements.

Cooperation institutions host regular EPNs. Employees look forward to them. When hosted in a tight 90-minute format – with a well prepared pacing – the reward of such events is long lasting and dramatic. Performance gains result from transmission of common vision. Renewal of common vision is required to maintain performance gains over time.

If the organization is a dental office or a congress person's staff – the Employee Participation Night – may be hosted – as a dinner – with a film and/or PowerPoint. Rewarding from the top down is a feature of EPNs that is a critical path to cooperation empowerment. Adopt the rule to praise by email and plus by phone or in person. Never correct by email. Reward in person in front of peers for maximum impact.

VISION PLANS – CREATE THEM & TRANSMIT THEM

HEART INTELLIGENCE

The Heart Math Institute in Colorado has long been an endorsed resource in our CEO trainings. CEOs who are in the know are increasingly learning better ways. Recently, we have learned that the main physical space that stores our memories and capacity to receive inspiration and to act on them is – for lack of a better phrase – "brain" cells that surround the circulatory system.

Super Achievers involve both the head and the heart decision making systems. The heart makes many decisions that are irrevocable – the mind never does.

All decisions of mind can be reversed and undone.

Many decisions of the heart are forever.

The brain surrounds your skull with energy fields that operate from twelve inches to two feet from your body – a powerful wireless device.

Your heart operates a measurable energy field that surrounds your body from sixty to one hundred YARDS and always from six to twenty feet.

While we seldom connect to one another's brain – we are all intuitively awash in one another's heart energy.

Heart Math has demonstrated, along with other studies they reference, that the energy fields from this enormous field generator – create a grid of overlapping fields (us) that encircle the space we know as earth.

Heart intelligence is documented study now taking place worldwide. We are discovering that there are two intelligences – mind or brain – and heart. The Heart intelligence may actually store the bulk of our experience and as an input/output device return the higher Velocity Acceleration and Momentum for the work product of original ideas. Original ideas are inspirations that surpass the total learning and memory data storage of a single unit (human) to develop. The new work product provided by such a unit (mind – body – spirit system) surpasses all the quantum theory known to man.

Heart intelligence may be the way "in" to the future. A growing number of neuro-scientists now believe that the brain's problem solving capacity has been exceeded by the global village environment in which we now find ourselves living. Professors such as Dr. Lee Pulos of the University of British Columbia are now investigating via bio feedback and related studies – whether the heart intelligence, as the fountain of original creative ideas, can be super stimulated to open itself to even greater performance.

Long overlooked by traditional education – the model of the past concluded that only the brain should be understood and educated. Today, the left and right energy fields of the heart – with its capillary system providing pathways sufficient to out perform brain density on an order of eleven to one – may provide keys to the future of our species.

One process leading CEOs are using is a simple check device that, once initiated, becomes a habit. The first point of self observation for the switched-on leader is to become aware that you are virtual personalities – a left-brained personality – a right-brained personality – a heart and emotional personality – a work personality – a home personality – a mom, or dad, or sister, or brother personality – a lover personality – a leader personality. We are all multiple.

When making key decisions – you might use critical space time outs – which can include a restroom freshen up –   phone & email free – quiet space – (It doesn't need to be long in duration). The heart responds to breathing –

A proven model is to shut your eyes and simply repeat – "my mommy and I are one" – which may sound strange but ancient avenues open as your measured breathing slows and you open new pathways. Become aware of your breathing.

As you do this first part – place your right or left hand (whichever you use to write with) over your heart and allow it to rest there. Both hands may be used.

As you complete ten rounds of measured breathing – place your calmer thoughts on the single focus of the decision of the moment. As you consider the decision – move from your head totally into your heart under your hands and simply suggest – "so …what do you think" …and be quiet and repeat in spaced intervals – "tell me" and relax and let your mind go blank.

The answer from the heart doesn't always come right away – so complete by saying "so tell me when you're ready" – and let it go – open your eyes and return to your responsibilities. The rule is the heart answer always WILL come however – and it won't take long. The more frequently you involve "whole-being decision making" the less time the answers take to reach the CPU mainframe.

The CPU mainframe recognizes the heart's answer as WOW. The heart's information is always a WOW.

As all teams work best with recognition – when the WOW arrives – remember to touch your heart area – and say …sincerely … "thank you." You'll begin to feel the power of this new behavior as you apply it. This behavior resolves virtually everything. The most serious financial, emotional, relationship, physical and related issues are resolved by the suggestion – "so...what do you think?"......

"How should I resolve this irresolvable issue?"

"Should I get a divorce, or not?"

"Should I do this, or that, with a child...what do YOU think?"

"Should I fire so and so, or hire this person, or that person?"

WOW will explode to your brain and your mind will instantly know the better way – the better resolution for what it is – and slowly – if you choose to work the process – your mind will open to the second WOW – as your brain will begin to know the source – and appreciate the team work –

Whole being thinkers are considered by society to be geniuses.

Every baby regardless of birth condition arrives as pure genius.

The heart is in full partnership with the brain at birth.

Slowly we teach our Super Achievers to forget their genius and to live totally in their brain or head.

We begin at very early ages to come from the head.

We reward head activity.

We become almost embarrassed by heart activity.

Still – all the creativity and genius – arrives as WOW exclusively from heart intelligence.

If you regard your heart as a simple muscle – why is the energy field surrounding this one muscle extending up to sixty feet from your body? What is the implication of the grid of our mutual wireless communications heart-to-heart – locally – globally? Is it worth further study? The medical doctors and leading physicists at Heart Math Institute have been bringing this new knowledge to the leaders of nations and business for the last few years. Click their website and search to gain the latest details and discoveries.

In shifting CEO leaders into whole being decision makers we have discovered a "short cut" for those open to the process – to massively elevate performance output in thinking. The most direct path to Super Achiever mindset (upgrading mental software) is through the Heart. The more you thank the heart intelligence (the alternative individual inside each of us) the more rewarding the heart resource becomes. Ideally, the heart and mind working together create the best Super Achiever mindset. Because this state exists only in cooperation versus competition it becomes the natural way for the soul to express itself in Master Manifestation.

Master manifestation is how we exist as children of God.

Until we discover our own masterful manifestation – we distance ourselves from the source. When we become more resourceFULL, or full of the source – we become closer to the source. The closer we become to the source the more PowerFULL, or full of power we become. The more powerful we become the more humble we are. The less humble are as far from heart intelligence as worm hole travel is to a New York Subway.

Truth is always compelling. The mind often can't see the truth when it's reading it. The heart knows the truth because it feels it. The great aspect of the truth is that it's scientific. The truth does not care if you believe it. The truth does not operate if you trust it. The truth repeats and exists every time you test the premise...is this true or not? The truth is repeatable.

While many advanced exercises exist in Heart Math practices for leaders and CEOs, the only ONE that is required is the mindset exercise we suggest in Super Achievers. Your decision – will be to test the truth. If you become full partners in cooperation with brain and heart resources – your life will demonstrate an output we call – miracles.

Super Achievers are manifesting miracles.

FOCUS

Another Mark of Super Achiever thinking is the quality of focus. You see focus as a challenge in young children today.

Alvin Toffler's *Future Shock Generation* is dealing with the limits of adaptive change. The reptilian brain is super stimulated by multimedia. Saturated with such stimulation the study habits of individuals are fragmented. Paying attention – the master quality of Super Achiever mindsets – is virtually impossible for the undisciplined mind. Mental conditioning on the topic of attention management is the foundation building block of Super Achiever mental states.

Individual minds demonstrate results from years of "working out" in the area of attention management – via the skill of being enabled to "hold attention" on virtually any topic for any time length desired. The wattage for such voltage is known as WILL. The Super Achiever can fix incredible attention onto or off any project at WILL. Others can feel such concentrated forms of attention.

Attention manifested in coordinated waves of energy – reinforce one another at the peak and trough of the wave and become cohesive energy – much like a high-energy particle beam of laser light. Attention is an energy wave. Fragmented, this wave spreads out such that less and less light reaches the target as time or distance pass. If attention is highly focused – as with sound or light – the energy becomes something altogether unique – no energy is lost as it travels to the target.

Weapon grade applications of laser light were developed at the turn of the last century by TRW. Prior to that the amplification of light was considered to be impossible. In the early part of the century, this changed the battlefield by being able to apply cohesive light such that enemy shells were made harmless. They simply could no longer reach their target.

Weapon grade attention projects focusing attention are under way in areas that include remote viewing (it works folks) and in structural damage to bridges and other objects – specifically from attention management alone.

Attention creates all the great enterprise employment tax base and evolutions for society. When Jack Kennedy using the antique technology of the time stated – in a single decade mankind will land on the moon and return safely to the earth – it was thought to be impossible in the time frame. However, the attention placed upon this single goal was so focused the objective was more than realized. Nations that focus attention progress as Super Achieving nations. Where nations that convey fragmented attention (uncoordinated thought) display fragmented output. Nations rise and nations fall. The rise and fall of nations are at core a feature of the "quality of thinking and the focus of attention" of the nation. The nations which are most free and cooperative tend to prosper over time where the nations that are more competitive and less free tend to decay over time. Cooperation is a display of highly focused attention; competition is a display of competitive scattered attention. Cooperation exists in confidence; competition exists in fear. Attention is almost impossible to focus in fear save for the topic of war at individual, organizational or national levels.

The skill of focused attention represents a breakthrough for students. When students pace the room and imagine they are taking out a video tape from their mind – a video tape that runs a show featuring how much they hate the topic of their study – how they can't and won't learn the study material – why they are blocked and so forth – and they imagine, as they pace, throwing this video tape in the waste basket. Still pacing, the students move to grab an imaginary replacement DVD or video and place it in the slot of their mental forehead and see it load and open and run that suggests – they really want to learn geography; they really want to find out some things about this study material; and they, with changed focus, return to the study position – hydrated – sitting in an upright, energetic learning position – begin to study – really study with some eagerness – attention is riveted on topic. Attention management is a state of mental discipline. Holding attention on topic is mastery.

Employers who review the work output of an individual from High School forward – can determine when the individual (if ever) mastered holding attention on topic – a feature of mental capacity. When seeking out teams the mind that is longer mastered in attention management is the superior teammate – following aspects of resonancy and like minded temperament. Become an evaluation machine for the attention management of others.

CEOs assess the attention management of others by listening versus talking. You will find that those who listen in return have superior attention management. Those who are myopic in focus – inward and on their internal agendas – without sensitivity or regard – for the cues that are being presented to them – are limited in their attention focus skills.

Attention masters understand non verbal cues exchanged by others. There are entire lessons on:
- Career cues
- Decision cues
- Team cues
- Church cues
- Family cues
- Relationship cues
- Leadership cues

- Financial cues
- Marketing cues
- Administration cues
- Threat cues
- Reward cues
- Correction cues
- Parenting cues
- Sibling cues
- Affiliation cues
- Recreation cues
- Social cues
- Missed cues
- Diversity Cues

Paying attention to the CUES of life is a learned behavior. Super Achievers are highly focused attention machines. Super Achievers are super sensitive to the cues of others – and seek out master trainers to increase their skills of mind in Cue Management Technology.

These lessons founded at IBI are rapidly becoming one of the sharpest new industries for global training companies. CEOs were quick to spot that training in Cue Management Technology, (CMT) delivers improved diversity resolution in the work place. IBI Faculty member John Gray in his *Men are from Mars and Women are from Venus* publications (for home and work) provides crucial cues for Super Achievers. Cue Management Training is becoming a multi million dollar industry –

All training of this nature impacts the ATTENTION Management of the aspiring Super Achiever. Altering the way an individual holds attention is a terrific effort. As with all such efforts, individuals are unlikely to retrain their decision process without expert help. Attention concentrators become the Super Achievers who dictate the terms of society in our Global Village. Paying attention to attention is a very smart CPU idea –

PAY ATTENTION TO ATTENTION.

SUCCESS KILLERS

Consider the five principle success killers in life:

1. Blame
2. Negative Self-talk
3. Procrastination
4. Fear (competition between brain and heart intelligence)
5. Victimhood (virus control of the CPU)

No way, that's me?...or anyone I know?

I don't recognize myself in those five items.

I can't count the breakthroughs I have witnessed as individuals identify the combination of success killer factors at work in their lives. One of the biggest steps to winning huge new results in your life is to become **open-minded** to fresh awareness of your own success killer combinations. New success comes by dispelling the success killers at work in your life, through recognition.

Success killers are habits. For most people success killers have become an all too comfortable way of life. The thought inventory you choose to hold in your mind has become habitually (automatically) reactive, by default to a combination of success killers – known as bad habits of the mind.

Success killers are viruses of the mind. We load these viruses throughout our lives from others who also have them – without ever knowing when we are under a virus attack. Super Achievers have carefully acquired better code known as "mental firewalls" that block and preclude hackers from placing unwanted viruses of the mind into our mental software. Our typical means of becoming infected with a mental virus is by wireless, high bandwidth transmission from others like ourselves. Weak virus programs become stronger in any of the five categories above – as various like minded viruses on topic – combine into teams and groups and begin to dominate the CPU which attacks thinking patterns. Once we allow a virus to dominate our thinking, we ourselves begin to infect others with our faulty belief systems. The virus (error in thinking) has become our own core belief. Super Achievers remain suspicious and open minded that their belief premise may and typically does contain virus errors. Super Achievers are always seeking a "better way" of thinking from any previous state. Super Achievers are never satisfied with their mental state. Non Super Achievers are satisfied with their existing mental state and go to great lengths to preclude software upgrades to the mind – a virus attribute. Error code is written to perpetuate itself. Corrected code is always seeking better code – corrected code remains fluid – error code remains rigid. Cooperation thinking is fluid; competitive code is rigid.

As the great Fortune 100 Company trainer, Dennis Deaton, suggests in his books and materials at Quantum Learning in Mesa, Arizona – "the dominant thought you hold in your mind will dictate the reality you express in your life" – the plural applies to thinking in general.

Dennis Deaton's teaching is a great item to repeat out loud – from a print out in your work area – perhaps the one value a reader takes away from *Super Achiever Mindsets* – "the dominant thoughts I hold in my mind dictate the realities I express in my life" –

Dennis is primarily about one objective – teaching the mind, heart, whole body learner that you have spiritual unlimited freedom to "change your mind" – and thereby alter your reality. Attempted alone – most will not accomplish it. Attempted in community with expert coaches – most will never fail.

The truth WILL set you free ....

CEOs already KNOW what they MUST DO to obtain more success. Most leaders have failed to master the KEY QUESTION:

WHY AREN'T YOU DOING THE CORRECT ACTIONS IN THE CORRECT SEQUENCE YOU ALREADY KNOW YOU MUST DO TO CREATE YOUR NEW REALITY IN LIFE?

Answer:	I don't know.
Response:	But.....you DO know, don't you?
Answer:	I know.
Response:	WHY DON'T YOU DO WHAT YOU ALREADY KNOW YOU SHOULD BE DOING TO EXPRESS YOUR NEW REALITY IN LIFE?
Response:	I'm not sure.
Answer:	But you DO know…in fact you have ALWAYS known…for…

Life is a school of self instruction.

Let's say you're substantially overweight. You already KNOW exactly what you must do to lose weight – in fact, you probably know more than the rest of us. From surgery options to group association and help, you already know what you need to do.

You know you will die so much younger if you do not make the right decisions in this area – you do not require that we tell you more on the topic. You know you fail to enjoy the new appearance that is hiding within you. You can phone the world's leading weight loss specialist Dr. Chris Spalding in Adelaide, Australia. Just one phone call to get started toward "the perfect YOU" hiding within. You will never put the weight on again. You will lose your weight for life. You will have a new image. A new you. You will live a longer, higher energy, more joy-filled life. In fact, you already know more about your body than anyone else can ever teach you.

You know, don't you?

So why won't you start?

Why don't you DO, what you already KNOW you MUST do?

The answer is typically universal –

"I don't know."

And the lesson of "why don't you DO what you already know you must DO" applies to any subject in life, when you desire success and deny yourself the pleasure of progress.

Success takes effort of mind first and physical action second.

Success on any subject is a consequence of a series of decisions that lead to action. Decisions without action are known as considerations. Decisions that lead to action are known as completions. Successful thinkers display more completion than non successful thinkers.

Improvement requires commitment, a decision in and of itself.

Success is never-ending and requires responsibility. You can't pass success off to your life partner, your best friend, your bishop or to any third party.

Sir Isaac Newton was so very profound with his 3rd law

of relativity in that it is so easy to fall back into habitual existence that a lifetime can slip by.

You and you alone manufacture each and every improvement in your life. The output of improvement in a single life is a contribution to all of us in the Global Village. When you hold back on yourself at any level of existing success (or lack of it), you hold back on all the rest of us. When you commit to greater success, you commit to all the rest of us.

You have discovered that Success is a learned behavior. You have learned that most people do not experience success.

You have learned most individuals fail to DO what they already know at a core level they should do – to acquire success. Why don't spirits do what they already KNOW they should DO?

Why?

Keep in mind the majority who become *SUPER ACHIEVER thinkers (the retrainable alive at any moment) did not get to "it"* until after they turned forty years of age. In fact, many of life's Super Achievers were dismal failures earlier in life. They had to LEARN successful thought patterns – more successful decision streams. Success is not derived from luck. Success is not an accident. Increasingly, greater success is a way of thinking. Success is not being at the right place at the right time. Success is the application of specialized knowledge (creating Multiple Income lifestyles like all wealthy men and women) and then sustaining application of the new knowledge through HIGHLY ORGANIZED activity (activity = decisions well made) with intention to higher contribution for all of the spirits in our global village. Your life thrills you when you internalize this principle. Competition becomes a failed organizing system inside you and outside you. Super Achievers seek out the systemic tools of retraining and reorganization into cooperative models – that breed lifetime growth in all areas of the living experience. There is no finish line.

Anyone can learn to THINK more successfully – and everyone should no matter how successful they are at the present starting point. The time to improve the process for making decisions is the instant the idea crosses your mind. Place your hand on your heart and ask for help. Place your hand on your heart and invite your head and heart to have a conversation (perhaps the first awake discussion in this lifetime) and suggest – "will you help me become a whole being learner?" See Super Achiever thinking as a consequence of whole-being mental activity.

WHOLE-BEING LEADERS LEAD COOPERATION INTO THE GLOBAL VILLAGE

To begin living life as a Super Achiever - you must rob the power of the five success killers from your life. The virus removal program starts when you become aware of which of the five are operating on your brain's CPU.

I wish I could list all the excuses for Blame I receive in my email:

"You just don't understand how he abused me."

"You can't know this level of betrayal!"

"I was put in prison for something I never did."

"She cheated on me when I was true to her."

Nothing robs people of success like the love affair individuals hold for dwelling in a state of blame! I've suggested to Jack Canfield and Mark Hansen that *Excuses for the Soul* might be a great title – appealing to tens of millions. However – paying attention to the problem, as "my father" taught his nine children – only manifests more problems. Dad used to teach us – that the magic is moving attention onto the solution rather than the problem (as their *Chicken Soup for the Soul* work has done so well)

– with the result becoming – RESOLUTION. Hold your attention on the solution once you know the problem – and you breed solutions versus more problems. This secret is worthy of a note to the office wall – with a thank you to the late Alan G. Dohrmann for his 1950's instruction to his babies at the time.

Let's now begin to look at each of the five success killers – to define if they are active in pairs inside your life. If you don't find yourself in the examples, you're likely to discover someone you know hiding right in front of you. Shedding success killers is a habit of the Super Achiever.

Success Killers Are Viruses of The Mind

BLAME

The discussions I often have, while also learning from the podium on stage, with audiences all over the world include summaries like the following:

BLAMERS I HAVE KNOWN

"If you only KNEW.....what happened to me...what put me into this condition in my life."

"Mr. Dohrmann, if you could only FEEL what is going on inside me, what it IS that I am feeling as I describe the following events."

"If you could share my blow by blow description......THEY cheated ME......."

"The conditions made it happen."

"No one could have come through what I came through."

"You just can't KNOW, you just can't understand ..."

"It's worse than you thought. My story is unique. No one has ever had a story like mine."

"I've been through hell, and it's still going on. Oh, you

just can't understand...there is no possible way you could appreciate what I've been through."

Blame is like a fable, a magical story that like a fairy tale leads to a happy ending.

The happy ending is that YOU are not responsible for your life.

You don't have to THINK that everything that happens in your life is your own responsibility. You can accept it. You can reject it. You can move forward. You can stop and dwell on past events. You can focus your "divine" attention – the only aliveness any of us possess – upon memories of the past – or creative solutions of the future. You can focus on creative tomorrows or yesterday's memories. As with all "switches" of the mind – the choice you make to place your attention on one or the other defines you as a Super Achiever or something less. You can easily see which is which by "listening" to the conversations of others. Are they largely discussing the future and their entry into it – or are they largely discussing the past and their bondage to it? You can learn from it. You can change the future. You can blame others. Or you can accept life – noting some things happen that are good, some that are bad and there is a degree in between along the way. The only variable is your reaction. You can accept everything as a lesson – or you can reject everything as blame. One is insane - one is sane. One is reality, one is non reality. You decide moment to moment if you are insane or sane depending upon your viruses of the mind. You are free to remove virus code for better code (less error filled thinking) in the instant miracle of freewill and choice. Highly trained minds begin to see more clearly than poorly trained minds. Whole-being thinkers see more clearly than divided head and heart thinkers. Blame is the number one success killer.

But why? Why exist as a past dweller – memory thinker – on electrical firings inside our brain that are non reality to the present or future? The key TIP here – is –

No one cares about the past you dwell on.

The past is useless. There is nothing in your past that is going to make your future better. You may find this concept startling.

Experience is experience. You HAVE it. You can't lose it. You can't forget it. You can't learn more from it. You already learned it. You can't learn more. You can dwell in it – but doesn't that seem rather insane? Why would you? The past just **was**. Your present IS and your future soon will be.

Each one of us is fully aware of the lessons we need to learn from our past, once we learned them, at some level. We may be asleep. We may be more or less awake that all experience is a lesson. Your worst fear is best greeted each morning with open arms saying the words "ah, my dear dear friend….so, what do you have to teach me this day?"

At some level we already KNOW all we need to know from the past. We don't need lots of new reminders of what we did wrong or what we could have done differently. We each did the best we could at the time. We all learn along the way. We can't do better – because we are doing the very best we know how. All of us. It's perfect. All of it. We can't improve it. And yesterday is long gone. We already know the lessons of the past – been there – done that – already. And truly, we know it is US and not the other party that is responsible for our life reality. Blame is like a drug. Once you are on the addictive mental habit of blame, it is hard to switch off the next mind fix. You tend to share needles and surround yourself with other minds (virus-code-infected CPUs) that wirelessly re-infect your CPU. You reinforce the belief you wish to retain. It may require asking your team to "catch you" and remind you to SWITCH your mental file cabinet - to reorder your mind files. Teams that work in agreement to help one another catch:

- Thoughts or actions that criticize another versus plus others
- Thoughts or actions that bleed versus breed magnificence
- Thoughts that focus on the past (past dwelling) versus future planning
- Thoughts that focus on problems rather than solutions

TEAMWORK MAKES THE STREAM WORK

When you step outside the old heroin-like habit of injecting blame into your thinking streams - for even a few corrections, you will become drug free – as better code takes over. Switching is a great team activity for High Performance Teams – once the Super Achiever mindset has become a goal of thought for teams or groups. Teams agree on outcome – and support one another with better decisions to reach the objective – as completions rise. As you build the future, past dwelling and blame shed like unwanted clothes in the tropics.

You CAN BEAT BLAME. If you find blame is a comfortable, natural condition, fight the habit – as you discover how much blame you are thinking, feeling and speaking. Reflect in self observation that blame is weak code. Get better code. Most of us are spending far too much of our life dwelling "far too many hours" (squandering precious creative options) on events that took place in the past. The giant, creative, warp-drive engine of your mind needs to be realigned to focus its startling, unlimited energy (attention) into the future, the next thoughts, the next choices, the next decisions that create your reality. None of these decisions are influenced by or hostage to the past. Your thoughts about the past don't make one bit of difference concerning the future. You can change your view in a SNAP. The question is ....WILL YOU?

Only you can paint your own self portrait.

There is zero value dwelling on the past. Studying it. Focusing on it. Spending important time, precious time, limited time, on review of the past. You know everything you need to know about the past. So, let the past go. The only value related to past decisions is that without a change to your core process for making a choice – which is, in itself, a decision about the future – your past is likely to repeat itself. As your attention remains in blame on the problem – you tend to remarry the next abusive spouse. To break free into the relationship of your dreams – your thinking must change. Your self portrait must include new colors and hues.

The only thing about your life that means anything, or has any value whatsoever.....is the selection of decisions you will make today and tomorrow. Your future is based solely upon which decisions you make, and how you will make them. The PROCESS you use to make a choice or decision is your future.

The power of your future improvements rests solely on your skill in making better decisions one day at a time.

Make the first great decision: let go of the past as a feature of a mental software virus – especially when blame brings emotions in to anchor the bad habit.

Think for a moment how liberating and freeing this chapter can be. Forgive yourself. Forgive others. Give up all blame. Give it all up. Your fresh start begins with this single decision. A fresh start commences the moment you make the mental choice for freedom to begin using better code. Breed magnificence in yourself and others and think no thought that bleeds magnificence from any of life's experiences. Accept betrayal and unfairness as lessons, and react differently to them. **BECOME NON-ATTACHED**. Give up the past as a focus point for the attention of your mind. The past is a memory. The decision you make right now is your future. Your decision about the next second of your life is the only reality. You live now. You are alive the second you read these words. This is your only true instant of aliveness - and then the next that follows. Live in the future. Live at the time your decisions are being made. Be fully alive **"NOW"**. Use the now moments of life as a treasure. Be powerful, not powerless. Liberate your mind. Give up the comfort of "past dwelling." Evolve into the creative, powerful, free, useful, unlimited personality you were born to become. Life is about becoming. The best you can become remains one decision at a time in the future. Our best work is ahead of us, not behind us, true at any age as long as you are alive. All thoughts to the contrary represent virus code.

The past has no power on your decision-making, or your future, unless you choose to let it. You can choose to reduce your speed of manifestation – it's always a choice. You can choose to dwell on the past. Recite the litany of BLAMERS we presented in this chapter - with your own additions. Say them all with feelings.

Or give them up -

The choice is yours. How you will live the rest of your life depends solely on your WAKE UP CALL to the awareness that power, real power, is an option. Your option, on how you select your mental inventory. The file cabinets in your mind are yours and yours alone to keep. You have the pink slip. You have the deed. You have the combination to the safe deposit box. No one, but no one can get in - to be inside the privacy of your mind with you, unless you let them. And you control what you put inside the privacy of your own mind. Most important you control what you KEEP inside this unlimited vault of possibility. And the OPTION remains – you and you alone can SWITCH to better code in the space of a SNAP.

Your heart and your brain can become your super networking team – in a SNAP – as whole being thinking begins – and cooperation thinking becomes the dominant thinking pattern. Reflection – self observation and care in team support – supply the tools. Expert coaching and training speed up the process of reprogramming the upgrades of mental software.

Nothing can effect your decision to CHOOSE to enjoy a blame free life. You alone eliminate blame and judgment through a process of thinking known as "hard work." Choose to enter a new mind state. Do not judge others. Do not blame others.

Life just IS.

Things just happen. You can choose to remove yourself from events that do not support you.

"This no longer serves me well."

Move along into something that WILL serve and support you. Insist upon positive future events, relationships, and results.

Deny time to blame, judgment and review. Forget consequence. Events happen. Deal with them in your most positive judgment-free, blame-free manner. Learn from them. Learn how you can avoid events that do not serve you well, and keep adding events that will positively nurture your future. Focus on solutions rather than problems.

Agree that the worst betrayals of your life are simply spirits who are too mentally damaged from virus code (too deaf, dumb and blind) to realize how much – how truly deeply – you have loved them. This, in the end, is your pain. Defocus on those who need you (the deaf, dumb and blind) and focus rather on those who are like you – those who can, with better code, speak, hear and see – choose those who DESERVE YOU versus those who NEED you. You can surround yourself with the neediest spirits – and enjoy maximum pain – or you can surround yourself with the most awake, deserving spirits and experience the greatest joy – the choice is always yours and yours alone to make.

Like pearls on a mystical necklace, add perfect pearl after perfect pearl to your life necklace as a matched set of more perfected decisions. Situations, career opportunities, team members, friends, life partners, and so forth, which WILL support you, are all decisions. You are never stuck based on old decisions. You are never trapped based on yesterday's choices. You can take any pearl (if it is tarnished or damaged) off your necklace and replace it with a higher quality pearl (decision).

You can stop the sadness of the way the pearl once was, by focusing your child-like thoughts on the new pearls (choices) yet to come. The new pearls you have yet to add to your necklace – the new choices – always elevate the mood of every child "inside." There are always delightful new pearls to add to the necklace of life, if you will only lift up your thoughts to joyful, playful, innocent, child-like enthusiasm for the possibilities yet to materialize into the reality you are creating. You and you alone create your reality.

You can change anything and everything. In a single SNAP of your decision process. You are always one single core decision away from hope, from enthusiasm, from happiness, from joy, from health, from companionship, from love, from perfection.

PERFECTION "CAN" BE HAD – SEEK IT OUT

Make today the last day you allow blame to kill your next success. Accept responsibility for your life choices without blame for anyone or anything. Blame is INSANE in the new millennia. Blame is boring this year and next. Blame is a yawn you'll begin to discover as you see others trapped in Blame. Note: Choose teams that are blame free already – for individuals who are virus infected may choose (and often do):

...to be unteachable at the moment....
or that you are not their teacher.

Accept life. You only have two choices. Reject lessons (continual turmoil) or accept life (blissful living). Choose to accept everything that has happened in your life as lesson. Forgive everyone that has ever entered your life and hurt you:

"FORGIVE US OUR TRESPASSES AS WE FORGIVE
THOSE
WHO TRESPASS AGAINST ....US!"
"FORGIVE THEM FATHER – FOR THEY KNOW
NOT WHAT THEY DO"

Pretend you face an eternity, being judged and in that moment you wish to not be blamed. You step up to the bench. You will now be judged, forgiven for your own injuries to others, for the way you yourself forgave. Are you ready to face this type of pure judgment? Being judged and blamed the way you do it today to others? Accountability in cooperation does not create blame. Accountability requires performance that is steadfast and a feature of positioning. Everyone needs to be positioned to a place they prosper and are sustained. If your performance fails to rise you probably require repositioning.

Even if you don't believe in God, by the way, the words above still work. The famous Twelve Step story:

A man is working on high rise construction during the evening pick up, and falls over a high beam.

As he's holding on with one hand, the beam begins to slip.

Although the man does NOT believe in an all powerful source of life, he calls out: "Oh Lord, please tell me what to do."

To his amazement a booming voice answers from the sky, just as the beam is slipping more.

"Yes, My son, I am who that I am."

And the slipping man cries out, overjoyed, "Lord, tell me what it is that I am to DO?"

The voice replies "Let go of the beam."

Stunned, the now panicked man looks down and says:

"Lord ,did you say let go of the beam?"

To which the Lord replies, "My son, what you must do to be saved, is let go of the beam."

The man in desperation cries out one last time:

"Is anyone else up there?...........'

You can't have your positive future, while you hold mind inventory of negative indwelling on past, on blame, on judgment. The condition of the mind that delivers these mind inventories is habitual. Until you discover "non attachment" you will struggle with blame. To remove the blame habit you must recognize mind virus code exists in the first place. When chronic, multi-virus programs dominate your thinking, you will need expert help. There is plenty of help if you will only ask. However, it is hard to let go of the blame beam.

If you see chronic process in this habitual area, commit to fix the problem the first time you recognize it. Get help and do it fast. Phone now. Network. Get referrals from friends. Remove blame, the success killer, from your life. Let your Golden Circle know you are working on it, and have them catch you when you fall.

Clean up your mental inventory. Make a decision to begin.

Stop giving time to thoughts that lead nowhere. Stop investing time in thinking about any past area of your life, as comfortable and habitual as it might be for you to do so. Make daily efforts to increase your alertfulness. Recognize thinking about the past, and SWITCH your mind to think about the future. Force yourself to dwell on making a better future for those you love (in all your relationships) be sweeter and more considerate as blame free patterns take hold. All those you come into contact with are "doing the very best they know how" – they can't do better – their mental software controls their output – and they may not understand how to upgrade. Forget and forgive everyone and everything. You don't have to tell them. You don't have to communicate or share life with them. You simply must forgive them.

Give up blame.

Force yourself to dwell on making a better future for everyone you work with (career partners) for your dreams, for your destiny. Stand for nothing but a future you insist, regardless of the fears and doubts, is more perfect.

PERFECTION CAN BE HAD........you alone decide

FORGIVE YOURSELF FOR EVERYTHING

NEGATIVE SELF-TALK

CEOs are the file clerks of your own mind. During your life the "on-the-job training" you received for the file clerk position was pretty shabby. We all had limited training related to THINK-ING. We all received minimal self programming skill and virtu-ally no decision reformation education. Yet, these core skills limit or expand our freedom in life to the exclusion of all other skills we learn. Why then are these master principles of mind not more widely associated with public education? CEOs might begin to express a need for decision reformation training – in all education. Your work place would flourish with such a focus.

The accidental default trainers, your family, your friends, your career associates are simply not experts on the subject of mental software – for they, themselves, are largely untrained and populated with virus code they inherited long ago. Lacking proven expert trainers, the mind accepts by default the only train-ers it can get – providing a maximum of mental virus code to the perfect CPU technology of the Global Village.

The mind will conform to the reality that surrounds it and adopt the code of this environment. However, one must note the secret truth of all advanced spiritual study:

YOUR REALITY IS A CONSEQUENCE OF THE DOMINANT THOUGHTS YOU HOLD IN YOUR MIND.

Most people fix this axiom into their mind in the reverse. You gain beliefs not as a "SO." You hold them as a list of "SO"s that you have accepted in your life. You may not remember why you believe the SO is actually SO. However, the belief is real and the reality is SO for you.

You just know that the reality is SO.

A friend was talking with me in Phoenix, Arizona recently having gone through Avatar Training from Florida. A real estate sales professional at the time, he described his experience.

He went on to tell me he had envisioned a clear calm pool of water...a tiny lake alone in the mountains without disturbance from any human condition.

During his mediation he asked his mind to pull forth his true inner belief on the subject of relationships. And he had the word SUCKERS arise from this ancient dark pool of the mind

He was surprised about this, but his instruction said he could not touch or alter the feeling or visual word, with any preface.

In discussion with others in the room, he realized, at a deep fiber core level, that he DID hold the belief anyone trusting in relationships (whether spouse, career, friend, etc.) were indeed SUCKERS. His protection mechanism was fully formed.

His conscious awake mind (the golf ball on the EPCOT CENTER) tried to talk his subconscious mind (THE EPCOT CENTER) out of the concept. The notion was not the self image the golf ball (his tiny awake mind) was holding of itself. The notion was not the self image the awake personality wanted.

However, the deep-within personality (the larger Epcot Center of the subconscious mind) held fast to the belief as this feeling was indeed SO for the individual.

Trusting, loving relationships were only for SUCKERS!

The very awareness of this condition began to change the individual as recognition for a mind virus took hold. Recognition is the first phase of virus removal.

My friend said he felt a huge shift inside himself. Within his body. He couldn't explain it very well, but he felt the shift. He felt it like a physical thing. It was emotional. Yet, Real. And tangible. A SO was departing replaced by better code. A new SO was arriving. Beliefs were changing. It was a core reprogramming decision. A better code decision.

More important, he learned something from the experience. He could feel his belief (now illuminated with recognition) dim to the more enlightened acceptance of his far stronger desire for a different future by holding a belief that relationships could be for WINNERS rather than SUCKERS. He retrained his subconscious mind to replace the old reality with a new reality, that FRIENDSHIPS COULD BE HONORED HERE – at the core level of his ancient spiritual lake. He made a heart and mind decision – a whole-being reprogramming decision – and for a moment in time – experienced the mindset of the Super Achiever.

He told me it was like a light going out – when the old SO departed. A light he could feel. The old belief was just extinguished. It felt so huge when it vanished like such a relief. He asked why? He felt the void like a darkened room sweep over him. He also felt uplifted and improved.

I explained that the effort to attach versus unattach requires enormous strength in the form of distraction. Attention is distracted from its purpose – and the result is always estrangement from core truths to replace virus mental code. The relief comes from the letting go of the tension to attach to the virus. The virus is preserved by attachment as with all parasites. Viruses are parasites of the mind.

There are two projects that consume a lifetime for the serious student seeking the Super Achiever Mindset. The first project is the work of never-ending upgrading for the software of the mind – as we develop recognition (file clerking) for the thoughts we hold in our minds. **The awareness we choose to develop defines us as Super Achievers**. Stand back one nano second and see, "Is the thought or feeling I have been holding this instant the quality of thought I want to keep? Will I make it a SO in my ancient lake or will I recognize the thought as a virus and refuse it room at the top of my mind?" Displaced thoughts (unattached) wither and die. Will you replace the thought with a new better code that illuminates your mind with the decision stream process of the Super Achiever? A conscious priority to work on your mental decision process is the choice of elevated consciousness.

SNAP AND IT IS SO

Habitual self-renewal of this nature is a learned CEO skill set. The skill must first be learned personally, typically with expert help and then resolved via group reinforcement to become habitual. This SUPER skill must next be practiced to be enlarged. The Mind is muscle and the sit ups most required are TEAM MEETINGS with Like-minded Partners and expert coaches, all guarding their mental file cabinets – all in agreement the Super Achiever mindset is the state of perfection desired.

Super Achiever teams express themselves as breeders of magnificence with every person, circumstance, or action. Teams that bleed magnificence from others represent competitive models that will always bow over time to better code. One way of thinking always leads to war – the other to peace. The Global Village has completed investing in the failed thinking of war as a resolution recognizing such thinking patterns as virus code. Nations have virus code. Super Achievers adopt the axiom every nation is doing the very best it knows how to do – at the time it is doing it. What is SO for a nation may rest on a virus.

Nothing is written to your MIND disk that cannot be replaced and rewritten. The program supervisor is you. The password to get into the high security area of your disk is the skill of expert recognition. CEOs or nations can learn to recognize the virus code that creates the SO conditions of their reality. Every old SO can be deleted and replaced with better code. Is it loving, generous and kind? Is it selfish, fearful and greedy? Is it magnificence breeding in all expressive forms or is it magnificence bleeding? Is it filled with blame or is it blame free? Cooperation vs. competition is easy to recognize. Begin to make it SO in your own thinking.

Once you have recognition of a mind stream you will wish to proceed to the more advanced exercise in the discovery of "hidden files" on your computer storage disk. A computer program has hidden files that help to operate your computer so that you can perform tasks. These SOs are buried and take further effort to discover.

Your mind has hidden SOs stored in your deepest self. Discovery of the beliefs that you have adopted – that define you – can be such a surprise, as it was for my friend in Phoenix when he felt the word SUCKER attach to every relationship in his life.

Why?

The conditions that make your life "SO" have originated from many non experts, who have been default trainers passing on their own viruses of the mind in a never ending circle. As we fail to educate our young concerning mind skills, such skills typically develop only late in life – after often tragic histories of applying error code time after time after time.

Sometimes the hidden files are spewing forth rejection. Perhaps, life injuries that affected your self-esteem or other emotional pains run quite deep. Why? Because you and you alone let it, because you have been untrained and because the pain to review the virus is so intense – you refuse to even talk to yourself about it. The abuser spouse keeps abusing or drinking or otherwise gaining the permission they require to retain their misery. The primary SO is that the thinker is NOT responsible for the reality he experiences.

The things that are SO in your life often come from others, many you may have forgotten or never realized their impact. SOs that linger forever if hidden and undiscovered operating your core CPU. SOs that dictate your self respect, your ability to love yourself, forgive yourself, improve yourself, and give unconditional love and support to others. SOs that rob you of life.

The lack of training allows "virus damaged decision streams" to make it SO real for you, when as you obtain new masterhood, the incidents that bothered you at one time of life, can develop a smile at another. How many Hidden files are so buried on your hard drive CPU that you may not find them – alone - ever? What a trap to fail to self discover – the virus protection program – keeping individuals from their own self discovery.

TIP: Search for leading training classes that teach decision reformation trainings. Become the best mental file clerk. Spend a lifetime attempting to master the secrets of this one mind skill. Invest your life improving the way you clerk the file quality of positive, wholesome, uplifting thoughts inside your mind. The slip stream of your mind is the place from which all altitude sources. Eliminate judgment of others as an extension of blame. Cancel this fun and habitual program that grounds positive thinking.

Eliminate the pleasure and habit of dwelling on the past. Replace this old program with the new thinking habit of forcing your mind to dwell on files (thoughts) of the future, of increased decisions, of better decisions. Be thankful all the time for your FREEDOM to make so many new decisions and to always craft your future.

Success is the distance of the smallest fraction of a degree of greater self perception coupled to action to intervene into the decision stream of your mind.

SUCCESS IS A STATE OF MIND

CONSIDERATE LIVING

Considerations inside the mind lead to the habitual life of procrastination. Procrastination is epidemic in the world population. Our way of life is threatened by the lazy person's guide to self improvement.

Consideration of a subject is NOT decision-making. The huge bulk of failure activity in life is tied to the wrong reality (belief) which has become a "SO" for too many individuals:

CONSIDERATION OF ANY FUTURE POSSIBILITY, IN-CLUDING SELF-TALK TO SAY I'D REALLY LIKE TO DO THAT IDEA OR THIS ONE AS A GREAT COURSE OF ACTION – BUT YOU NEVER ACT – IS CONSIDERATION. DECISION WITHOUT ACTION IS CONSIDERATION.

Consideration is risk free, because there is NO ACTION. Consideration leads nowhere.

Millions invest their life, convincing themselves that they have worked so hard making so many decisions that they actually feel that decision-making has aged them prematurely. They are literally POOPED from the process of making all those decisions along life's way.

They plop down in the front of a flickering cathode ray tube, (not so mildly hypnotic) and spend hours working it all out inside their minds. Between snacks, during commercials they continue to consider what they are going to do with their life. They consider the future all the time – they'll report to tell me. They'll consider this plan or that plan and keep considering it. Consider this action or that action. Consider everything and anything, over time, of course – over years, typically. Consider success. Consider tomorrow. Consider why it hasn't worked yet, and why it won't work probably. Consider the new plan for the new product, new packaging, new pricing, new personnel, new division, new global expansion – new ideas.

I'm considering starting this new job or business.

I'm considering stepping out and really improving my team.

I'm considering investing to attend this life improvement class that can upgrade my day-to-day living experience.

I'm considering getting married.

I'm considering changing my job.

I'm considering moving.

I'm considering getting help to stop caffeine.

I'm considering leaving my spouse.

I'm considering losing all this weight, really I am. And I will.

I'm considering getting my drinking under control.

I'm considering DOING something with my life.

Life just happens to me and I am considering taking charge of my life.

There are thousands of considerations. Considerations tire out the thinker putting all the effort into self-talk and procrastination activity. Procrastination is a harmful brain chemistry that leads to "dullness" of mind.

The only thing that matters in life is what action you decide to take. Decisions are expressed by action into completion. No completion, no decision. Even the lack of making a decision IS a decision. What you say, even privately to yourself, doesn't matter a wick as a loop of consideration – if there is never any action. The only thing that has value is the action you take.

Make your actions well intended, kind and generous to others.

If you are POOPED from making all those considerations, realize you have wasted years and years of living through the lost decision points in time that have been mismanaged forever. The mind habit of considering action is epidemic. A horrible bad habit for humanity brought on in part to these epidemic proportions by the television generation – the modern Roman Coliseum.

How many television generations are there?

Answer.....ONE! You are the first.

Television is BAD for your mental health. Television is more powerful and damaging than caffeine or most addictive drugs. Just try and get off television.

All the way off.

Try and return to higher mental values of reading or conversation – and witness the withdrawal you are likely to move through.

Television involves light energy, color energy, hypnotism, altered consciousness and seen and unseen mental stimulations. Just try and tell someone that their dinner IS ready - to test this theory - while they are watching their favorite series. Television lowers awareness as in self perception.

TELEVISION LOWERS AWARENESS
AND STIFLES THE CREATIVE
PROCESS OF SPIRITS

America has lost the competitive edge everywhere in the world; the competitive edge that we owned everywhere in the world until the 1970s. What changed things so dramatically? Remember we lost our position because the other nations (without television) developed better ideas for such items as lap computers, automobiles, and even big screen television sets, better car designs, better everything designs – and the result – WE BUY FROM THEM – hence the balance of TRADE in the RED problem. In the boardroom of the mind, we have lost a race that can only be restored inside the unlimited potential of the mind.

From 1970 forward America spent more money on prisons than we invest in public education. Every nation has entered decline from Greece to Rome to the USA when the national output begins to place more resources into incarceration than education. The process can be reversed but strong national will is required once the decline begins. Fear often blocks the expression of such will. Ignorance of the core issues also blocks improved decision making for nations.

Using fear as a tactic – and tough-on-crime politics as the new welfare in the USA – over 500 civil matters are now criminal when previously such acts where not considered "crimes." The list is growing.

The Federal Bureau of Prisons has moved from the smallest of Federal Agencies prior to 1970 to the largest and the fastest growing. Just over a decade ago when Bill Clinton took office the high for all incarcerations was around 800,000 total – including state and federal – even then, it was the highest in the world per population. Today almost 3,000,000 are warehoused in prison – primarily for non violent, victimless crimes – with new super long sentences for relatively minor offenses – with an entire industry base supporting this policy as a new form of state welfare. Prisons supply slave labor now "leased" out for private industry.

Meanwhile education has been reduced to a class of services that fails to teach our young to even read or write. As a dollar transfer idea – we might wish to move our prison population into new services for society. RETRAINING might be more important than "RESTRAINING" for the large majority. Think about the cost to freedom and society by the trend of spending far greater percentages of GNP for prisons than for education of our children.

Financially and nationally what we are deciding to do now – reduces our national interest to a low point we may have no recovery from. Think about your own role to reverse the trend. Math does not lie. The jump from 800,000 prisoners in the USA to 3,000,000 has not lowered the crime rate. Switch the channel if you don't like the program. It might be that the decision process in this area of human resources requires some fine tuning to Super Achiever mindsets. Countless lives are lost while we fail to educate, retrain, and advantage those who make the most poor decision choices. Better decision making is a priority of national interest.

Television is one medium that has led to a state whereby the USA spends more on prisons (the mark of a nation in decline) than America spends on education.

But television is only one culprit and there are many to share the blame.

Once again, leaders must adapt to the priority idea IMPROVE-MENT IN LIFE requires new learning and improved decision making. This is true for the most successful CEOs who wish to tune their mind technology – their core capital. If you really want to enjoy the fruits of the living opportunity in the shrinking global village to its fullest (and there is NO TIME TO WASTE as "now" is the perfect time to do so) you must first adopt the mindset that downloading frequent upgrades to mental decision making software – is life's primary opportunity and your personal new priority. Upgrade your mind annually.

This book is a giant opportunity call for generations of leaders in the shrinking Global Village. Your decisions related to on-going mental retraining can alter the course of history.

Take the step to make the most important DECISION of your life. DECIDE that you will transform considerations that delay action into more powerful decisions that complete action – reducing forever the stillborn decisions in your life. Considerations are replaced by resolutions – completed decisions.

RESOLUTIONS ARE COMPLETED DECISIONS FOLLOWING ELEVATED PERFORMANCE AS RECORDED BY INDIVIDUAL OR COLLECTIVE VELOCITY ACCELERATION AND MOMENTUM TO THE SUPER ACHIEVER MINDSET – KNOWN AS RESOLUTION FLOW DYNAMICS

You will learn new skills for action completing to the decision process as you practice holding Super Achiever principles in your mind. As you become aware of each principle – each built upon recognition of the other – going backward is far more challenging than progressing forward. You will adopt and nurture the Super Achiever mindset as your norm, a lifestyle that suits you because you are more awake to the methods of doing so.

There is one magic rule for making decisions: DO IT NOW!

TIP: *NEVER PUT OFF WHAT CAN BE DONE IMMEDIATELY – SPEED IS THE NEED – IN THE DEVELOPING COMMUNICA-*

TION AGE

Never delay in making a decision when you have the option of making the decision right away. Decisions without action leading to resolution are weaker. Resolutions are the consequence of more powerful decision making and display Super Achievers who are more powerful decision makers. Make the decision, then move on to the next priority. Reorder priorities frequently.

SUPER ACHIEVERS REORDER PRIORITIES MORE FRE-QUENTLY THAN NON SUPER ACHIEVERS

When a decision requires lots of information to make the FINAL decision, make lots of decisions to get the information required for the JUMBO DECISIONS OF LIFE. Your next decision may be to speed up your own decision process. Make decisions about how to evaluate quality at the time you expand the quantity of your personal new decision stream.

Speed is a feature of masterhood in decision-making. The consideration-driven mind produces results 1100 times more slowly than the decision-driven individual or organization. Paradigm shifts may overrun your business, your life, your marriage, your family before you make the key choices required years ago. Retrofit your mind and warp drive your decision process with absolute quality control on each decision made. Your plan for upgrading the software of your mind (via annual retraining) becomes the core platform for Super Achiever teamwork in any workplace or personal life.

CONSIDERATION/PROCRASTINATION is a mind disease. The way to get well is to get help, as with any illness. You cannot cure consideration illness alone. You will require help and lots of it. There are many fine companies instructing individuals in HOW TO start the process.

DO YOU HAVE CONSIDERATION ILLNESS? When will you seek professional help to secure the cure?

Landmark's Forum personal leadership training is one starting point. PSI Seminars (over 30 years of helping improve decision making) is another very advanced leadership dynamic training. Thousands of such programs are provided by professional firms listed on the Internet. In most cities, these firms can be found in the telephone directory – Tony Robbins is in San Diego and PSI is near the Napa Valley Wine country.

Every day take a personal inventory before retiring to sleep. Recent studies indicate the early sleep period is when the mind records into deep memory new learned suggestions. Learn to make powerful suggestions (hand over heart - beaming suggestions in also helps) to record to the super conscious "YOU" – just before you sleep. This habit expands resolution development – for the Super Achiever thinker and reduces considerations via deductive reasoning into core decision making.

Take only a few seconds of time to perform rituals of evening pre sleep suggestion work for your decision priorities. Ask for help. Review your day and reset future priorities. Was your day as decisive as you wanted it to be? When did your considerations fail to reach decision status via action? Can you speed up the quantity and quality of your decision making tomorrow? Night to Night the process of PERSONAL REVIEW provides accountability required of all cooperative systems. Review and correction mark the journey of the self expanding leadership. Self growth is the first growth. Every other choice comes second. Super Achievers make the act of self growth the priority decision.

How can you make more and better decisions tomorrow? How can you make better use of your time (a decision in itself)? Complete the mental pre-sleep review and commit the exercise to deep, worry-free rest. Whole-being sleepers receive amazing answers during their programmed resting via the power of suggestion. Make powerful suggestions – asking "how can I ....?"

just before you rest. Develop this Super Achiever "pre sleep" good habit. Have a note pad, so if you awake with the answer – write it down. You'll be amazed at what you record the very first week.

CEO TIP:

Try two weeks of pre-sleep work – and record the output gains that follow – when it comes to bottom line results – nothing impacts the bottom line – equal to elevated decision making.

Exchange your old habit of consideration for better habits of making decisions ONE DAY AT A TIME. Never miss a day of holding your process accountable via a review process. Develop this sleep time habit. And watch what happens inside your life as you record results. Resolution flow increases dramatically and immediately for all who apply this Super Achiever mindset principle. Remember not to spread the word. Your chosen associates may not be teachable at this time and you may not be their teacher – so take care that your pearls are thrown only to EAGLES of the mind (fellow Super Achievers).

For many are called but few are chosen

Cast your pearls only to the eagles in your life…unconditional support is a treasure too precious to squander…insist upon such support.

Report on your progress to High Performance Team Members. Invest in training from experts on decision-making education – to perfect your personal decision quality and quantity process. Months of old method decision making – filled with previously unidentified virus programs of mind – defeat resolution from manifesting completions over any time frame. Elevating the process leverages results. Retraining (upgrading mind software) elevates results. Virus removal elevates results. Virus programs return both in your personal work and in your team work. Regular upgrading keeps the mind software far more virus free when the output is measured in decision quality. A new priority for all human performance now includes frequent upgrades to mind software.

Nothing delivers success like a DECISION REFORMATION – such that the process for making choices has been improved – one individual leader at a time. The Global Village is vastly enriched as this process unfolds. Super Achiever thinking transforms the landscape of output.

Cut back on television. Watch as little as you can. Be far more selective to watch only programs that upgrade mental software and avoid mindless entertainment that infects your system with virus programming. Guard the programs of your mind and ask your team to do so too. Increase activity that fosters conversation via Super Achiever association. Read More. Use your Imagination more. Super Achievers learn to ration mail, television and online time. Ration all mail to Friday 9:00 to Noon – and your productivity will skyrocket. It's very hard – to reduce the allocation of time to "mind reducing" addictions – like mail – TV and online mindless browsing. Connect to one another in CONVERSATION – reduce non conversation time.

Make more decisions. Talk about positive mind inventory. Talk about decision-making achievements and the process of making better decisions CEO-to-CEO. Develop CEO associations that thrive on mental programming decision making discussions. Help cross mentor one another at the core CPU level.

CEO TIP: *CEO cross mentorship is a Super Achiever attribute – those who are proud and arrogant – display virus thinking .*

Develop a regular pattern of making your work of self improvement part of your out-loud and self-talk discussions. DWELL upon the principles of mental success first and the results of the right decisions second.

Check your thoughts. THINK BIG thoughts! Don't look for conversations of tiny detail. THINK BIG all the time. Enlarge your scope of contribution to the Global Village family. Expand your interests to THINK about global issues. Keep your conversations with others, your ideas, your habits of thinking on tomorrow, on the plans, on the future, on goals you seek to achieve next. Problems are what CEOs see when they take their mind off their goals.

Enjoy being in groups where the discussion is global impacting rather than inwardly focused to self centered small talk on items of the past three weeks of "memory." You'll quickly move more and more to the pier where the big boats (thoughts) are moored. It's a matter of choice where you dock your own vessel of the mind. Choose your slips wisely. Who you tie up beside dictates the terms of your safe harbor for life. Birth your thinking beside vessels of like size and quality.

Limit how many thoughts you will tolerate about yesterday, the past and all thoughts that limit the magnificence of others. If your thinking is not elevating the magnificence of others, you probably are dwelling on judgment, blame and the past three weeks or so of memory. Associate with those who focus on their future plans and actions versus memory dwellers. Limit time with those who focus on the past three weeks of memory with inward, myopic, self-centered words and discussions. If you're not learning Super Achiever decision making, you're just churning the possibilities via considerations. You're considering this or that. You may hold intent for a future resolution but you have limited power to act while in the habit of consideration as a state of mind. Time is squandered from the untrained process of mindless thinking.

Become more aware as you THINK about how your associations are thinking and if you are truly learning and truly growing in the presence of the words and actions of the teams you surround yourself with in life. Why live surrounded by other mind-damaged thinkers – all untrained magnificence bleeders by habit? Super Achiever discussions thrill you when you hear them. Associate with great words and great deeds. Each day make the new day better by choosing associations more carefully than in the past. Super Achiever association IS a learned behavior.

THINK Better thoughts, Bigger thoughts with care in how you choose the streams of thinking taking place week to week. Keeping a Friday Diary of the thoughts you maintained as your DOMINANT goals and self talk during the past five days of TIME – can do more to alter your future than any other act outside improving associations. Improving the DOMINANT thoughts we hold in our mind over a week of time – alters the realities we create for ourselves and one another. Society benefits when the dominant thoughts are more creative (exploring space) than fearful and destructive (war). The Dominant thought we, and our associations, hold in our minds dictates the reality terms of our families, villages, states and nations. Learning how to reframe our dominant thoughts requires instruction, practice, continued mentoring, and ongoing association with those making such aspects of living – the priority of reality management.

After all inspirations (as God's Holy Capital) are forever FREE, always unlimited and the source of everything "real" in life.

Thoughts are the source of your reality and everything that flows into your reality.

Improve your thoughts, improve your choices and you improve your life.

Improve your Decision PROCESS. Reduce your CONSIDER-ATION process and improve your life output!

IF YOU'RE NOT LEARNING YOU'RE CHURNING

FEAR IS MIND POLIO

A large power behind habitual consideration behavior is the power of fear. Fear is in part, but only in part, a learned behavior. We inherit instinctive, reactive fears to preprogrammed perceived enemies from our environment and surroundings. We learn to fear the personal injuries of modern society including emotional threats. The psychic brutality of rejection as one example; the self defensive posture of withdrawal; the safe harbor conduct code (of the mind) which leads to potential lifetime impotence for the Super Achiever decision-making process – is perhaps stunted in growth by FEAR.

Making a decision, any decision, (taking action) is the only path that leads to future consequence (RESULTS). Nothing grounds the energy of positive uplifting ACTION like fear. Fear is the natural lightening rod for the mind that grounds out positive useful energy. Teams damaged by fear can unravel substantial effort for Super Achiever creative engineering by creating fear for the outcome related to new decisions. The mind is conditioned to avoid risk and to recognize fear as a risk review process that can thwart new decisions. Action is avoided to reduce fear and avoid risk.

Fear processes affect not only your own direct experience but also the energy that surrounds you. You exist inside an interconnected energy field. New studies point to the conclusion that each and every human being senses the environment in which he/she lives (energy field) at yet to be discovered levels. Fears may breed in this unseen land of awareness.

We only begin to understand the natural order of the strongest emotive paths flowing from our fears, from our dreams, from the core imagination within us all.

Fear is also a primal emotion. Fear may develop, as with any natural storm, over time, as events dictate. Anxieties may unfold from frustration or lack of action (decisions) from prolonged consideration. Outcropping from guilt and other perceptions can increase fear. New challenges engender fear of the "unknown" even if the "new" is a great improvement to our lives. Fear blocks more completion for individuals, families, communities, states and nations than all other forms of human mental states combined. Fear can be natural or a man-made mind virus. The mind can't tell the difference. Learning to manage fear as a leadership mind skill requires formal training. Traditional education provides limited or no training on the key topics of human behavior related to team building, relationship quality control, and fear management. Lacking training in these vital topics, men and women are frustrated and find it challenging to support one another.

Early in life we each learn the flawed problem solving mechanism of competition. We are teased and belittled for reasons unknown to us. We discover that conformity requires false praise for low traits while higher traits are ridiculed. Most of us learn by age five to bleed magnificence from one another. We have never experienced formal training in how to breed rather than bleed magnificence with one another hence we find we feel unsafe in the presence of one another. We learn to fear one another.

Low self-esteem brings out maximum fear. Self doubt, guilt,

and other illusion or phantom mind conditions make many CEO beliefs or SOs the reality that breed fear. No matter how silly the SO we adopt, once adopted as a belief, the SO has the force of a falling ten ton safe. The impact feels the same to the believer even if the belief is unreal and untrue. It takes great power to overcome the illusions of the mind. Hanging around those who speak and know the truth (magnificent breeders versus bleeders) helps leaders remain in a mindset of discovery, where virus information of the mind is replaced with the truth or corrected programs.

Fear, regardless of the source, is a natural cleansing process. Action cannot be taken in a sustained, healthy direction for the individual when a fear attack is present. When we introduce the concept of a fear attack, we are not talking about the fears that protect us from harm...such as...The fear to turn when a car is coming into our lane....The fear to slam on the brakes...The fear to protect our infant daughter from the hot burner...The fear to avoid touching the hot pan in the oven...The fear to keep the hair dryer away from the tub...The knee jerk fears of natural protection...The instinctive fears of the night.

Rather, we are now talking about the overwhelming panics that develop from new experience in our lives. Leaders all know the penalty of being out in front. Leaders experience regular fear as they challenge old beliefs more frequently than those who follow. Decisions, when accelerated, always take us into new experience. Super Achiever mindsets represent natural states of being in which decision making is perpetually accelerated. The mind naturally fears the unknown. Any GIANT fear attack, for purpose of the Super Achiever mindset, is known as a FEAR STORM – and we all experience Fear Storms throughout our life. The final Fear Storm – the fear of death – occurs just before we let go and graduate.

The mind is most comfortable "considering" new experi-ence, while avoiding the action that will lead to the new experience, a decision. Avoiding future action and natural fears of new experience – is a condition known as denial. We deny the better software code for the mind – the better way, the truth – to avoid the fear we may be wrong in our own eyes (but especially wrong in the eyes of others) related to the life choices we make. We sell out our entire potential for our futures to the cheap ad-diction of approval and acceptance from others – the most fleeting of all narcotics in life.

Most people experience FEAR ATTACKS we call Fear Storms on a regular basis. Fear Storms appear more frequently if you challenge yourself to explore new beliefs more frequently. If personal growth in your own decision making has become a pri-ority in your life, fear storms are well known to you. Fear Storms generally come at regular periods of the day for most individu-als. For one person, the time of the fear storm may be every three or four weeks, at 2:30 AM in the morning. For another, the Fear Storm may strike in the late afternoon, or mid morning hours. Fear attacks follow a cycle pattern unique to each individual as a pre-set established at birth. Fear storms may come more often or less frequently depending on the degree of growth you choose to place into your life. Fear storms typically hit in a time com-mon for life, either AM or PM. Duration of Fear Storms is also typically fixed to individuals. One CEO may experience a Fear Storm of minutes – another for days. Each has their own natural pattern. Do you know yours?

Few people write down the time and dates of their FEAR STORMS. Start keeping a record of FEAR STORM activity. Record a personal diary each time anxiety of sufficient strength to be classified as a FEAR STORM appears in your life. Begin to define your own Fear cycle as a process of professional fear management. Fear management helps you define how many superior choices you are working upon. Fear management helps you lead as you experience far larger futures. You will learn a great deal of how FEAR STORMS operate as a marker for new experience you are choosing from your Fear Storm Diary. Record how long each Fear Storm lasts.

TIP: *Never take action when a fear storm is raging.*

The more decisions you make, the higher your self-esteem becomes. The more decisions you make, the less frequently you will experience more serious fear attacks. This rule may become true for you, following a possible initial period of increased Fear Storm frequency as your decision stream accelerates. Thinking this way is a learned behavior that is best practiced in a group. Fear Storms are natural consequences to the art/science of improving our thinking process. For a short time (typically 180 days) the aspirant to the Super Achiever Mindset may experience an increase in the frequency of fear storm activity, hopefully recorded in a professional Fear Storm Journal.

TIP: *Use a hand-written Fear Storm journal booklet (available at any Wal-Mart or similar outlet) – it takes only seconds to make your record – versus a computer entry approach. The Super Conscious mind processes hand-written information differently and more impactfully than CRT keyboard entries. Handwrite data related to fear storms that dictate your process of mind.*

Never underestimate the power of Fear Storms to road block future action. For many the Super Achiever life (dream) was derailed at one time or another due to Fear Storm activity. Anxiety may strike out of cycle, at any moment during the day from your normal cycle. Record such freak storms when they appear. You're getting closer to ultimate Fear Management as you record your own cycle and timelines for Fear.

FEAR IS A MARKER FOR PROGRESS ON THE TOPIC OF ELEVATED DECISION MAKING – ALL SUPER ACHIEVERS PASS THROUGH THEIR OWN TERROR BARRIERS.

Fear is impossible to eliminate for emotional creatures (humans). Leaders are not immune to fear attacks. No one will fail to recognize their own fear storm episodes as they become more self aware. Talking about Fear Storms within Super Achiever teams is a healthy outlet and tends to dispel the quiet period for making decisions and taking action as the storm dissipates.

We found, when IBI first introduced Fear Storm Lessons, that virtually no other entity had offered any formal fear training to leaders. Fear management is important. Fear is a new topic of study in the mind business and over a few decades we are seeing new offerings in the Fear Management area for CEOs. Fear Management is a training which is defining to great Super Achiever Behavior.

Information about fear is developing rapidly. The first professional course instructions on fear management are only now reaching the market. There is great need for this form of classroom for CEO leaders at the top – for only at a peer to peer level does fear-sharing on a Global Perspective assist the CEO in making future choice. Fear of hostile takeover, fear of positive M&A decisions – fear of regulatory activity – fear of numerous CEO at-the-top agendas, requires professional fear management to inspire superior decision making. Teams trained in Fear Management always make improved decisions over time versus those lacking such skills.

Fear Management is important in the work place, at the staff and employee level, because Fear creates much of the stress and related "off time" in the work place. Fear Management is important in the Boardroom. Fear Management is important in the bedroom. Fear Management is important in the family room. Fear Management is a learned behavior. Success is impossible without mastery in the proper application and use of Fear as a tool of propelling velocity, acceleration and momentum versus retarding velocity, acceleration and momentum.

Our team has labored for many years to help develop leading courses on fear management instruction both for business and for individuals. We now sponsor and encourage other educators to engage in this important field as the curriculum and skills training expand.

I believe a far more successful living experience is possible when fear is understood and channeled. Conquering fear (the old idea) is an unnatural behavior, and therefore does not work, but breeds bigger, more frequent fear storm activity. Who wants to increase their fear storm intensity? You cannot fight or vanquish fear storms. Fear storms are a natural body rhythm within every human being. Because they are natural, you will experience yours – whether you prepare for it or not, whether you manage fear or not.

Fear storms will come. They will pass. CEOs are advised to create new expectations about their own fear storms. CEOs are encouraged to understand more about fear and to develop a fear management strategy for their teams - as a propelling thrust to remain out front at the leading edge of global village leadership.

SHOW ME A LEADER OUT FRONT – I"LL SHOW YOU A FEAR STORM MASTER AT WORK

Fear STORMS are absolutely devastating to creative positive thought. Clerk-of-the-mind activity must be suspended during a fear storm. Fear Storms ground positive energy, neutralizing the results that creative, productive thinking would otherwise deliver. Fear Storms reduce the effective output of family – organizations and nations.

Fear Storms without awareness training, can lead to negative life-changing decision patterns. Typically, fear leads to inaction. Fear breeds impotence to the positive, productive decisions of life. Fear blocks to resolutions in life can become habitual for the untrained mind.

To DO NOTHING is itself a decision. For most opportunities doing nothing is worse than doing anything. Doing anything is better than doing nothing in most circumstances.

Fear makes us impotent and less powerful for no reason. Lack of understanding is the real culprit. When was your last class on fear? When did you experience any hands on fear instruction?

For most people the answer is never. Never in formal education. Never in the family. Never from circles of mediocrity. Never.

Yet fear and fear storms are a regular, recurring condition of life. Shouldn't we know more about something so powerful inside us? Isn't fear almost as powerful as sexual urges, eating urges and related powerful drives? Fear storms block out sexual appetite, suppress the desire to nourish, and generally overwhelm any other mind activity. Fear focuses total concentration on the DREAD OF THE MOMENT.

Fear is a deep, primal, human emotion. My father once instructed me on the truth already mentioned in this book, "emotions just come."

Emotions develop from another plane of existence and cannot be controlled by conscious thought.

With training you can control how you REACT to emotion. You cannot control the swelling up of the feeling itself.

For example, if you get angry, you will experience anger. If you are terrified, you will experience terror. If you wake up and have that special day of joy and love in your heart, you will experience bliss. If you feel depression hitting you in the face you will experience depression.

You can do nothing about the experience of the feeling. The feeling will just come. The feeling is natural.

The feeling of all emotions is key to our full existence in time and space as spiritual beings. Feeling all human emotions more fully is the completion of "being" human. Emotions are the key to commitment where conviction turns desire into reality. The process of experiencing various emotions checks upon our values and beliefs to secure a condition of alignment. The alignment we ourselves decide upon, knowingly or unknowingly dictates the terms of our entire fabric of reality.

Fear Storms just come. You can't stop Fear Storms. You can't win by fighting them away. Fear storms are the giant storms of emotions that wash over all of us from time to time – typically when making some of our best decisions related to future action. The top prize winner in doubt is the consequence of unmanaged Fear Storms. The top prize winner in terror and mission impossible to our heart's desire is unmanaged Fear Storms. Fear storms just come.

The storm may be small or it may be very large and run on for some time. The storm may last a few minutes or a few hours. But typically, not a few days. However, unchecked, misunderstood FEAR STORMS can be addictive and like blame may become a norm to the living condition, an unwanted virus of the mind – a bad habit. Individuals in such a state are phobic and require professional support to recognize the magician's trick for the illusion which Fear Storms are - bad habits of mind require virus removal to load new "upgrades" to the existing, flawed software. Phobic Fear Storm activity is rare and manic and requires outside help. Attempting to develop better mind patterns for phobic Fear Storms without outside help is quite rare.

Most adjusted individuals will nevertheless be immobilized at times by powerful FEAR STORMS in life. Everyone reading these words understands they are gathering new truth, which is absolutely vibrating inside them at some level, and recognizes the information as useful. Understanding, especially new understanding, is the most powerful human ingredient besides more love (the software of the heart) that is worthy of our Super Achiever living experience.

The mind student should keep the thought, "all fear storms pass." The fear storm is a type of entertainment to the master of the mind. The Master permits the storm to roll upon them as a decision aspect, prior to action, that completes the decision/resolution process inside our minds. All the while, the Master is aware the storm is but an illusion. A part of the natural order. A testing ground for new behavior – new experience – new action.

The Master Knows the fear will lead to a cleansed new day. A day within that has recharged many cells within the body and spirit. Notice how strong you feel AFTER a fear storm. Notice how well and vibrant you feel once the storm has passed away. As Fear Storms pass, "quality" upgrades take place proportional to the power behind your action/resolution progress. As you move into completed choice – action – and display new language and movement – action – the quality of resolutions that move your future into desired new reality manifest. Master manifestor thinking is a quality of Super Achiever thinking – impossible without fear storm management skills.

During a fear storm, Masters make an adventure of their worry. Like a bad science fiction movie, Masters play out the illustrations they are receiving. Use the fears to weight values and beliefs to see what you wish to hold onto, and what you wish to let go of. Always know the play of fear is an illusion. Reality is a product of your conscious choices, not your emotional reaction to considerations. Regard your reactions to the flow of life events as your most important mental asset when developing Super Achiever thinking skills.

Flow with the fear storm. Don't resist it. Flow down the road, no matter how terrifying, to see what it would be like to really be that scared, to really be that in danger, to really be out there that far. After, you may have trouble even remembering details of your journey. You will feel a keen sense of being refreshed. Why? Fear Storms rebuild the internal filing system of the mind. Fear storms help strengthen resolve and motivate future action. A Fear storm is usually the final indication you are ready to make your decision by taking action and moving ahead.

Fear can be banished by using exercises of mind to shorten the duration of the storm. A simple mind/body exercise is the single best fear switcher. The exercise works as follows:

- Allow the fear storm to roll upon you solidly.
- Let the fear storm keep you awake or torment you for as long as you can stand it.
- Eventually, you will tire of the effort and want to switch your mind from left or right brain activity to the alternative brain dominance to eliminate the fear.
- While lying down, stretch your hands and your feet, so that you maximize a full body stretch to the point where you actually are shaking with the extending effort. Hold this position for five

to ten seconds, or as long as you can. Pretend your body energy is flowing like a shockwave - sweeping through you and away from your hands and feet out into the universe. Really release as much energy as you can, stretching so hard you are shaking for several seconds.

- Let the fear flow from the middle of your body up and away from your hands and feet. See the fear shooting away from you and notice the energy shift in your entire body after you relax.

- Hold your ear with opposing thumb and forefinger – pressing on the lower ear lobe (cross-handed in the ideal) while in recline – elevate the tongue to the roof of your mouth – squeeze the lower ear lobe – right hand left ear – left hand right ear – counting back from ten. Repeat twice.

- Now hold your inner fleshy area between thumb and forefinger – and with tongue elevated to the roof of your mouth – squeezing to create pain – and nerve flow blockage – this second whole brain balance mechanical activity – is fear storm blocking – count back from ten.

- Repeat once every thirty minutes if needed, three times maximum. The exercises reconstitute right/left brain imbalances and create a more moderated normalized brain function. Fear Storms act like giant electrical storms in the mind and are, in part, grounded and normalized by the whole brain normalizing exercises set down in this section. For Fear Storms that interrupt sleep – these exercises typically return the affected Super Achiever to normalized sleep – all without waking up a life partner.

Typically, one energy shifting exercise is enough. This energy shifting exercise will shift mind dominance from one sphere of the brain to the other, virtually eliminating the offending Fear Storm energy. The mind shift exercise can be employed anywhere, anytime. The best use of the exercise is while resting preparatory to sleep, following a bout with unpleasant, unwanted emotion.

Fear is not the enemy. Fear is a natural processing device of mind. Fear management strengthens when applied. Educational programs on Fear Storm management can add skill to assist Super Achievers who wish to develop greater mastery in Fear Management technology.

TIP: Never make decisions when in a fearful state.

Always remind yourself that the fears you are experiencing are balancing emotions and are NOT REAL as relates to outcome. Fear is an illusion taking place only inside the mind. Fear is not what's happening to you NOW. You are NOT EXPERIENCING what you "fear" in your thought. The fears you allow to flow over you like a rainstorm, are simply unwanted possibilities you are dismissing, not holding onto, which like any storm, pass and are gone in a short time.

Your reality flows from decisions you are making next. No decision you have made in the past binds you. The decisions you make next bind you to your reality. Your choice concerning how you will react to fear is one of your most important life mastery decisions. Study and learn more about fear. Never tire of gaining new skill and expertise on the subject of FEAR MANAGEMENT.

In the future see Fear as a giant movie. Watch the most terrible images on the movie screen you can experience. Your spouse dies. Your child is injured. Your business fails. You lose your home. You are ill. These are terrible, awful fear-thoughts. Then take the image that is too terrible to view, and blast your huge movie screen with a blaster device you hold for just such a purpose. See your movie screen fill with light as the screen dissolves and even brighter, white light from behind the screen fills your reality. The new white light is healing, and more bright and wonderful than any light you have ever known or seen. No fear can exist in this bright, whitest of all white lights, which flows and pours into the area around the screen of your mind. Healing you from fear. Lifting you up. Showing you laughter and replacing fear's foolishness with confidence, certainty and conviction.

Burn every corner of black, then imagine white light so no border exists except in pure, white, loving, brighter-than-reality light. Light that sweeps you up and holds fascination for you. Concentrate on the light and how white and colorless the light is. Where did the light come from? How is the light possible? Feel the difference?

As you learn new mind skill to react to fear in exciting, personally empowering ways, you will free yourself to experience success. You will move through the obstacles that challenge the strength of your new commitment to be successful and actually experience success. Nothing will stop you. Nothing will hold you back.

Once awake, you will never fall back to sleep again...the golden rule of awareness.

Fear Management is an important skill to master for the soldier of personal awareness. Each bout with fear is an opportunity to improve your management skill.

A final gift of your first exposure to fear impotence removal, concerns the words in this book. These words, once understood, can never be unlearned. You will never again experience fear in the same way. Never. You will now be free in life in a way you have never known before when making tomorrow's choices. This primary decision gift is eternal for the Master of fear. Gift wrapped by your growing awareness of who and what you are. You are an existing or a developing Super Achiever with a mindset that is focused on your core objective – of "thinking."

You can never unlearn your lessons on thinking skills. Can reading a book forever change your mental process to a more razor sharp focus? The final test will be at the time of passing or at life graduation. You (and all the rest of us) will pass this test in a new consistency of joy and anticipation as you blast your fear away to experience your true being. There is nothing for you to fear as a spiritual being of unlimited love and potential when you graduate. The only real fear is ignorance. Your commitment to ever increase your field of illumination (learning) will leave you with more love, more education, and more personal power as you approach your graduation. These treasures go with you when you move forward to enjoy eternity with one another. Once you graduate all the magnificence bleeding of the world seems so silly and slow as you enter the total magnificence breeding of your graduation class.

Frozen light will unfold and the thaw will begin.

VICTIMHOOD

Victimhood is different than blame, but frequently hires blame as a joint venture partner. Victimhood is a way of life. Victimhood and martyrdom are methods of living in a state of ongoing insanity. The Victim is temporarily or permanently insane. Super Achievers experience the Victim state with a power drain and become fatigued. Super Achievers can't change the path of the unteachable – Victims typically are addicted to their core state.

The insanity revolves around the self-inflicted delusion that the victim is no longer directly the source of his own reality. This false premise is, by its nature, wrongful thinking. The file clerk of the mind is out to lunch. The out-to-lunch sign may have been hanging on the door of the mind for a very long time.

Super Achievers find victimhood boring. Listening to repetitious renditions of why a person's life has done them "IN" is truly boring for the more awake mind. What is wrong with this picture is not only the rule; what is wrong with this picture is the entire picture. Avoid mind pollution. Surround yourself with Super Achiever mindsets and your planet shifting journey has commenced. The victim finds you boring because you WILL NOT participate in his blame game.

Let's say you're in jail, but you're innocent. Let's say your life partner cheated on you, and left you. Let's say you lost your only child. Let's say you are wiped out financially because someone cheated you out of all your money. And so on and so forth.

Or let's discuss that a virginal nun delivering medicine to the children of a South American country, Sister Mary is jumped near dawn one gorgeous morning on the jungle trail, raped and killed. She is twenty years old. Pure. Innocent. Unprepared. Victimized for sure. Brutal soldiers left her terrorized and dead. She did not deserve it. She had dedicated her life to serve others. And you are her mother. You are blaming God while playing a lifetime victim role. You tell everyone how could Sister Mary, your daughter, have been anything but a Victim. The Victim misses the point. Sister Mary is a saint – and the mother has become the Victim.

"Oh God, why have you allowed this to happen? The bible is impossible with the reality of my baby girl so violated for doing your work. You cannot be what I believed in for such a brutal rape and murder to exist in the world" and so forth, and so on – with many variations included along the way for seasoning to the Victim Soup.

And, of course, your life as a victim has all but stopped in the process.

Super Achievers don't believe in the random theory....Chaos theory. Super Achievers believe the source of all creation "I AM THAT I AM," **IS**. We believe all that we are this instant remains and always shall exist as the holy IS "inside" regardless of flawed thinking and the outcome of lower quality thoughts. Lower quality thoughts can not affect higher quality thoughts (thoughts of the Saint). The Saint forgives the Roman soldiers because.....they know not what they do...they live deep within the Victim Soup and can never know freedom. The Saint is always love filled and virus free. Freedom is a state of mind.

Super Achievers believe that a free will demands eddies in the stream of creative conscious behavior; as all forms of creative endeavor struggle to flow back to an increasingly closer relationship to the creative source (in awareness). Awareness is a personal Gameboy that never runs low on batteries as you play your own game. Awareness is a one operator Gameboy. Each plays his own game and records his own score. It's more fun to play by those with similar scores. We call angels Super Achievers. The natural order is the most exciting of all games; we call this game Life.

Reality, like emotion, just IS. You accept or you reject reality. There are no other options open.

Dwelling on the events of life that have gone by forces you into a "reliving loop." You sadly relive life in a never-ending loop of revisited experience. Typically, living in denial of past realities – a state familiar to the lifetime victim.

As the perennial victim is reporting on the rationale for accepting the victim's story (approving it really) and a Super Achiever is typically mind yawning privately, until the SA is almost thinking WHO CARES? Who really cares how you "react" to your own life experiences? We all have great days. We all have great challenges. It's all an adventure. No blame. No judgment. No victims. Yes, there can be accountability – and those who operate below social standards (violent criminals) can be held accountable for the thinking error. Increasingly, warehousing flawed thinkers is a victim mindset – versus the Super Achiever mindset of reprogramming the error thinking as the root cause. We can erase crime by elevating social thinking. We can never erase crime by reinforcing the thinking errors through wholesale warehousing of the victims and non Super Achievers together. How could such a game plan work to benefit the world?

No one cares, dear, about your indwelling on past experience – your personal victim stories. Such thinking errors create nothing. Such thinking adds nothing in life. It IS nothing! We don't care about your betrayal. We don't care about your lesson plan and the hard lessons inside. We all have to go through them. We do care about your RESPONSES to these life events. While we are happy to provide empathy for any experience, Super Achievers can't endorse victim mindsets.

My advice to the victim is short, sweet and to the point.
- Get sane where you are insane-before it is too late
- Accept reality. It just IS.
- Switch your mind to hold thoughts about future decisions.
- Stop thinking about the past; it doesn't matter.
- It just doesn't matter. Let go.
- Forgive everyone – forgive everything – unconditionally.
- Get help if you need it – get help fast.
- Hang out with Super Achievers to stay well – Super Achiever mindsets self correct one another in the most positive, sweet manner.

You are not a victim by birth. You are a child of God by birth. You have an immortal lifeforce operating inside you – we all do. This power operates flawlessly whether you believe and know about your core program or not. You are allowing the source of all creative power to express infinite experience through the personality that you have selected to become. You are always becoming more than you were yesterday. This progressive condition of the human living experience is unstoppable. Thinking errors are preventable – with great focus at all levels of education on thinking and decision reformation training. The mind loves to think. The entire system loves to improve quality to the thinking process. Freedom is a consequence of mastery.

You are lousy with denial if you are a habitual victim.

You are incapable of forever remaining ignorant of your true nature regardless of thinking errors. Your motherboard is hard wired to the source. No virus can ever affect the circuitry of the motherboard.

Your mission is to wake up by loading upgraded mental software.

Give recognition to every shape you see as a consequence of infinite intelligence. Receive pleasure from the universe in every thought you take. Become blame free. Become victimless.

Create the power of attraction into your life and display your personal power of magnetism.

Build your future upon a dismissal of the illusion you are a victim in any aspect of your life. Test and correct more quickly. Your personal pop quiz develops from decisions as events flow around such higher choices. Super Achiever mindsets connect the flow of events in life to the earlier decisions selected. When such awareness rises, the games really begin. Reality just is. You don't LIVE your LIFE in the past hour; you LIVE your life in THIS hour and the NEXT choice. Choose to live every thought for its best and highest good. Victims are selfish. Super Achievers are generous and kind.

Success is a consequence of forgiveness.

Victim free living is a state of choice. Victims often learn their pattern before age 18 and lock into the pattern as a frozen stream of decisions. The Victim reality is broken by right association of higher quality thoughts. Self awareness is required. Letting go is required. Super Achievers should only teach Victims who ask for help. Spend no time instructing the unteachable.

For the unteachable, just being "near" a Super Achiever is sufficient. Being "well heard" is cathartic to the incurables. You help the incurables – and there are millions – by listening to them and by loving them.

You teach yourself in the process of the healing you apply by being, rather than doing.

Teach only those who request your instruction.

Learn to take "care" in who YOU request instruction FROM.

Choose the higher mind with love.

Victimhood can be shed like an ancient snake skin that no longer serves a purpose.

Super Achievers wear new skin to surround their new Mindsets. You can see them in all their shining glory – not a victim among them.

SUPER ACHIEVERS UPGRADE THEIR PROGRAM OF MIND
AS SOON AS BETTER CODE BECOMES AVAILABLE

CAPITAL

Most people have dreams. If you create ever-improving Super Achiever High Performance teams you will enjoy more dreams (team dreams) than you can implement in your life. The passkey to success is to adopt sequence for output. Success is sequence for creative thinking organized in Free Enterprise principles.

CEOs require capital to develop any idea, new division, merger, acquisition, or growth, into a full blown reality. Capital to create an office. Capital to complete the idea development. Capital to market the idea. Capital to manage and administrate the idea. Principal Free Enterprise skills include:

- You must make it.
- You must form a distribution plan for it.
- You must market it each month.
- You must administrate it.
- You must capitalize it.

Capital is the big mystery in our society. We don't know why. The rules are easier today than ever before – yet we never teach at MBA level – any of the core freedom rules of the capital game. Why does a free entrepreneurial society fail to teach those coming behind (the next generation, our entire future) the rules of the capital game?

Capitalism is not a political system. Capitalism is a description of our way of life. Our standard of living is built and maintained upon free capitalism. Yet most CEOs cannot even describe capitalism.

Democracy is a political system. Capitalism is a way of life, derived from a financial theory.

First rule: anyone in the Free Enterprise World can raise "unlimited" capital. You can start today to lay out your capital plan.

Most people can raise enough...of Dollars, or Euros, or Yen following a simple TEN-DAY LIFE SUCCESS PLAN...even if you have never raised a dime before and you work the entire time at another full time J.O.B.

You can become financially independent in the process. The only skill you require is HOW to take action from your capital decision. Capital is the tool used to make virtually any idea useful to the rest of us in society whether it's – printed – e-delivered – multimedia created – or otherwise. Capital is required as a tool – a useful tool – to wrap ideas in success clothing that permits the idea to be of higher service to greater numbers of people. Without capital, idea benefits are limited. With capital applied, idea benefits can become unlimited. We are damaged from false ideas related to capital and our output is limited as a result. Capital is in natural ebb and flow. If one were to embark on the most ambitious human endeavors – say to build tourist facilities in Space and upon the Moon while mankind mines the planets – capital would flow from where it resides today into the vacant space of NEED created by the original concept as well as the benefits of the original idea.

Financial freedom is a wonderful consequence of the Super Achiever Mindset. Super Achievers naturally yearn to have their ideas benefit more and more people. Plenty is never enough. The leaders in Free Enterprise always want to improve their "game" of social services. Everyone can enjoy a state known as "increase" related to financial freedom. Every village. Every location on earth can live for "increase" when Super Achiever capital rules are applied. The only limits are inside the mind.

We will now discuss developing capital for any new concept. You will pay yourself income from the moment new capital is paid into the new venture as CEO or idea originator. You will always pay yourself first. This Free Enterprise Journey will test each of the new SKILLS OF MIND we have introduced in *SUPER ACHIEVER MINDSETS*.

You can pick up *Super Achiever Mindsets* at any future date, anytime you wish to move forward in life and BEGIN AGAIN. *Super Achiever Mindsets* never gets tired. *Super Achiever Mindset* skills never get sick. The message contained in *Super Achiever Mindsets* can be TRANSFORMATIONAL. You will never UNLEARN that which you have mastered.

Now, moving forward together, let's grow wealthy with one another in an ever shrinking Global Village of humanity joined forever in travel on spaceship earth. Let's move forward to protect our spaceship environmentally, as well as the coinhabitants we share the spaceship beside. Let us not lose one more species through past virus code within our collective thinking. Every "thing" whether plant, animal or mineral represents capital circulating through our traveling spaceship earth. We alone sit on the bridge at this hour. It is our watch. The crew, with improved training, can enjoy a far superior ride for themselves, as well as all the passengers they serve on the mothership earth as she flies through the stars. We have so far to travel. We have so much to learn.

The following steps outline how to raise unlimited capital. In the pages which follow, we unlock a mystery that retards real wealth creation for most individuals who desire greater freedom and success in life.

First, embrace the idea that owning your own rights and business is wealth creation and everything else is wages. You become full partner within the system when you serve on the board and own stock in the venture you work within. If you are only earning wages – begin to spot opportunities to fully partner by adopting projects to add value till you can own substantial stock (wealth) as well as serve on the board (idea directors).

Second, make the personal commitment that nothing, but nothing will stop you in your decision to INCREASE your service to others week to week – thereby increasing your wealth. Super Achievers do not remain static in income, social position, or service to humanity. Super Achievers live in a state of perpetual system upgrade – a state of INCREASE.

Third, never, ever, give up. The French gave up in Panama. They had lost over 20,000 workers to "yellow fever." Their idea was that mosquitoes did not carry yellow fever. Their investors went bankrupt from the virus idea held in their mind. Americans came in with a mindset of Increase and virus free. Soon there was no more yellow fever in Panama. The canal employed 54,000 workers and was built free of corruption, as a public service, under budget and in less time than predicted. Increase is a state of mind. Anything is possible if a small team agree on the ideas of Increase.

To begin a new division or Free Enterprise Protocol for capital, you will need the following tools:

1. Bizplan Builder Software for a business plan creation.

(Available at any software store). Chairman Burke Franklin is on the board of our super teaching public charity and a dear friend. You'll like his software.

2. A Mastermind Success Team, your Golden Circle. Resumes attract dollars – a good rule to keep in mind.

3. A capital plan – coupled to a legal private placement memorandum detailing the plan – for each capital formation – meeting state and federal regulations – (Click www.sec.gov in the USA for sample documents and regulations.)

4. Sequence – projections and budgets to sequence the new idea – division – or service into reality on fixed timelines.

5. A capital team to refer investors appropriate to the Capital Plan – such that the entire offering of your stock – or debt – to acquire the capital – is placed and sold out in less time for less cost – as your team makes the dream work. (Acquire Super Rush Seed Capital and Your Magic Folder from the ibiglobal.com website for step-by-step methods and procedures.)

With these tools you are ready to begin your journey to manufacture the success you desire.

Let's make a sample plan for raising over $800,000 of new capital for your pretend project idea. Together, let's pretend we have studied the private placement rules (www.SEC.gov) that exist for selling stock to individuals in your area (your state department of corporations publishes local rules online). The rules differ state-to-state. You will require professional legal advice before you proceed to accept funding in all cases. However, you may not require an attorney to begin, although you will want advice at some point.

It may be more efficient to prepare your new capital offering using new computer programs (several hours of work via jian.com) and then have an attorney review your "draft" document for a discounted fee. CEOs and their teams can prepare such offering formats tailored for individual modeling – from one million to billions of dollars. Securing an investment banking expert to assist with the engineering of your offering details speeds the process along.

Keep in mind, in a desktop publishing age, you can buy brand name law at Wal-Mart prices. Prices vary by vast percentages and work quality varies little in today's capital marketplace. Shop wisely and obtain discount law for your capital application.

Anyone can legally start up a new venture in free nations globally anytime he or she desires. In a growing number of nations you can incorporate online (see incorporate.com) for very small fees – automatically and instantly.

Work with lawyers who positively resolve problems, Super Achiever mindset attorneys. It might be smart to have your attorney read *Super Achiever Mindsets*. Avoid attorneys who make you feel defensive and who suggest problems for which they are the exclusive solution. Work with lawyers who make you feel strong and powerful about the plans and actions you are taking.

Someone on your team may know an attorney who would be willing to join your team with the most positive mindset. If you find your lawyer is hard to reach in a communication age; fails to keep you fully informed; provides work that is always last minute – switch lawyers and retain new blood. Upgrade quality; never settle for standards that are out of synch with your own standards.

Try to arrange a sweet legal relationship making your life easier. Watch for the slow lawyer. So many will eat time up like it was an unlimited virtue. Hold a stop watch when dealing with work from any professional. Develop:

- Written outlines of all work phases
- Details to be performed should be expressed in written agreements
- One fee for 100% of the work, no add-ons – no surprise charges – flat rate for project work is the ideal form to shop for
- A time commitment. If the work is late, the fee goes down. No exceptions. Time IS money. Late work or unsatisfactory quality will create "options" for fee discounts to the client side. If your attorney will not engage with your firm on such terms – hire another law firm.

If any professional makes you feel defensive, intimidated, or otherwise uncomfortable SWITCH law firms. Work with personalities that make you FEEL strong and powerful. Many lawyers have forgotten they are hired to tell you HOW to do what **you** WANT to do, not to tell you WHAT to do. You already know WHAT you wish to do. You're the CEO and idea source - you are asking the lawyer to avoid revisiting the WHAT as CEOs are paying attorneys to rush the WHAT into a legal FORM, so the HOW is in full compliance. Keep these references handy when hiring an attorney when capital or virtually any subject is the issue. Let your lawyer read this section.

If the attorney is "client control" in mindset versus "customer service" in mindset – hire another law firm. Be like minded with your law firm first, and only proceed with written engagement letters that detail the foregoing points second. Long relationships are founded on early understandings.

TIP: Following the reading of the foregoing information, proceed to ask the lawyer "Are you the professional I am looking for?" If they are offended with all sorts of details as to why these directions are off the mark as they explain what you require from their vision of the relationship –SWITCH law firms.

If they smile and say, "You know what, this makes sense. I think I AM the professional you are looking for." Smile back and say, "let's review the work, fees and timelines shall we?" and get both set in writing. You're in good hands.

CAPITAL IS UNLIMITED - THINKING CAN BE RESTRICTIVE

HIRE A LAWYER YOU CAN LOVE

One attorney will indicate you must pay them $25,000 to obtain what is called a Private Placement Memorandum to sell stock to raise capital. Another will do the same work for under $10,000. Shop. Quality is not sacrificed by smart buying for professional services. SHOP.

You will require legal support as a Super Achiever lifestyle takes hold. Seek out Super Achiever lawyers. They are everywhere.

Another attorney may do the SAME WORK for $7,000 but take $1,000 down, and payments for the balance over time. Terms can be as important as price. As to what the price and terms will be for the work, let the attorney know you are shopping for BOTH price and terms with a fixed timeline for performance.

As with any item of quality you "get what you pay for." If you desire speed you often pay a premium to get the speed. However, it is always time that is the most costly item. Invest in quality and speed. Be clear in your written work-for-hire agreements. Make them simple and easy to understand.

You may find another attorney will do the work with zero front-end fees, and take a fee with a premium when the project is funded.

Still another may work on your Mastermind Team and perform a preferred rate billing as suggested.

A private placement is a form of presenting the venture full disclosure approved by regulatory agencies. The form is a model CEOs can download at anytime for free from www.sec.gov, a legal form that is on a computer. You can buy software (BizPlan Builder is only one of the suppliers of sample forms at www.jian.com) which furnishes templates. It's simple and fast. There is NO MYSTERY or SECRET to presenting information about your ideas inside a FORM designed to permit free people in free capital societies to raise unlimited capital inside a system known as Capitalism. It's a basic freedom. Because we fail to instruct our young in these aspects of Free Enterprise or Capitalism, super creative adults are largely doomed to lives of wage slavery. To become a full partner with your system of FREEDOM, retraining is typically helpful. Much retraining. You can obtain everything you need to know for FREE from the Security and Exchange Commission of the Federal Government (ask for private placement rules) and from your state department of corporations (same request).

The form complies with government rules that note you MUST tell a new investor all the details they should know about your new business, including the risk factors. Full disclosure is the primary purpose of the rules.

Today, programs like Bizplan Builder offer computer versions of the private placement memorandum in template form for around $100.

Someone on your team should possess the experience to help you develop your legal capital documents using the new software that makes access to capital so much easier. Capital is your right. Any idea expansion can be funded in ten days or less with a little training on capital formation. For larger funding requirements, the time frame may be 180 days or less. Investment banker agreements increasingly should contain time quality control criteria – given the fees paid for investment banking and venture funding. Without a fee performance agreement there is lower quality to the funding every CEO is relying upon. Capital is a tool. CEOs rent the tool of capital to perform work output. There is unlimited capital if the rental firm (capital) is approached with reasonable rental documentation. Everyone can learn the money rental terminology for his/her scale and size of project.

In the new global village there is always a potential to reduce the time and cost of capital rental – and knowledge becomes most powerful when it is communicated in warp drive fashion. Systems that slow knowledge (especially related to capital) are stagnant systems compared to those systems that speed up capital resources. Capital markets are widening. There is more capital year-to-year in more new forms and on greater term and selection plans than existed in the years before. Capital buffets are offering Super Achievers better tools at lower costs to manifest their ideas. Society benefits when laws that speed the cost as well as the flow of capital upgrade on a regular basis. Yesterday's laws stigmatize a capital nation with old software that requires upgrading to remain current in the global village of tomorrow. Capital is the master resource Super Achievers cannot afford to be in deficit of.

In most states, you can approach 35 individuals who are not millionaires to raise seed capital. Venture firms and investment banking firms help fund second round or second stage funding. Such firms seldom provide capital for early seed stage funding. CEOs typically offer a private placement of a security (any agreement between your firm and investors) to acquire early seed capital. It's simple, but it's never easy.

CEOs can approach virtually an unlimited number of wealthy, sophisticated investors using 506 security law exemptions in the

United States. Local law firms can advise you on particulars for a one or two hour briefing on the rules for your location in the Global Village. CEOs can raise millions, to hundreds of millions of dollars of early round seed capital by offering capital providers stock, debt, or a combination of both (debt convertible to stock) as your next ideas are developed.

For $500 or less you can incorporate your new business in most states by completing a simple form the state will send you for free or better yet click www.incorporate.com. Online attorneys will instantly guide you through any road blocks. Just call your Department of Corporations in your state capitol and ask them (no attorney required). Investment bankers help you with the structure of your offerings – as do investment banking law firms.

The State will issue a stock minute and corporate book to you. The stock book will contain shares that you issue like a checkbook. Money you receive from private investors is paid into your new company checkbook. You may use the money immediately to pay salaries, bills and related company costs, including the cost to raise more money. How you plan to use the proceeds of investor capital must be fully disclosed; the details must be carefully represented to investors before they buy in to your project.

It is illegal to print money. It is NOT illegal to issue stock. You may set the value that you wish to sell your stock for in a free and open marketplace. In a new company the price of your stock relates to the value of your idea and other organizing factors, including your board and team, your demand issues. You and you alone can DECLARE the value you wish to place on your stock based upon earnings. The stock certificates appear like blank checks in your stock book. You issue stock like you issue checks.

CEOs write in the name of the shareholder and the amount of shares their firm is now transferring to the shareholder in exchange for capital. You are not in debt. Your sale of equity for capital is a RIGHT that you may be unclear about. Your formal education may limit your capital RIGHTS. What you don't know can limit you from capital markets. If you THINK you are not talented at music or the arts, the artistic side of you may, as a potential, remain unrecognized. We can grow our artistic talents. If you think you are unqualified to develop unlimited capital you can rely on the axiom "your mind will ALWAYS make you right." Super Achievers question their core beliefs on a regular basis. Super Achievers explore upgrading belief software, exchanging limiting beliefs for true freedom of upgrading to unlimited beliefs. Any belief that limits you is not a SUPER ACHIEVER mindset. Such beliefs can be replaced by upgrading the software of your mind.

CEOs typically ask for and receive legal help in keeping the minutes, electing a Board and so forth, but all of it is really easy to do. Computer programs can help you do each step without an attorney. PC Attorney contains most of the forms and costs around $100 to acquire $50,000 worth of legal documents and information.

Let's review the Capital Mindset and CEO rules.

- CEO completed a simple form to incorporate your company division or outlet for the new idea to the world. You organize every idea to serve more people using Free Enterprise Software (organizing principles) and capital.
- CEO elected to authorize 5 million shares of stock in your new company (as an example).

- CEO kept most of the shares for yourself in exchange for the idea (intellectual property) and work you contribute to the company. Investors pay in start-up capital as your business plan calls for.
- CEO prepared a private placement offering and/or a business plan and a stock offering form for an investor "magic folder" that conveys the details to the capital providers.
- CEO had a lawyer review your documents (your magic folder) and help you make your folder comply with the all applicable regulations.
- CEO offered stock, debt, or a combination of both to investors, using a plan we will explain.
- CEO raised more than $100,000 in ten days or less. You pay yourself and you pay company expenses.
- CEO continues to raise a total of over $800,000 in two weeks or so, you develop your business to deliver the idea to more people, and you issue stock to your investors like you issue checks in exchange for capital contributed to help you exceed your goals.

CEOs can and should complete the initial capital forms without paying a lot of money to third parties – the education provided here tells you how to go about keeping costs down and speed up. Shop hard and/or do the form yourself or with a teammate helping you. Unlimited Capital simply is not that difficult. Capital is the risk reducer to every plan of bringing ideas to the world.

This is especially true for a new idea, with no operating history. There are hardly any details to report in your capital form. You are just starting the new idea. You are not raising round two, three or five. Every round of capital, as ideas mature, requires fresh plans when ideas progress to venture and investment banking grade of quality (reaching more people).

Capital compliance computer forms ask questions in simple English. You answer the questions and the computer turns out a form that meets the rules for a private placement with State and Federal Authorities. You are then able to go to work by filing the forms. Lawyers help you with the filings, which in a Fed Ex world are virtually overnight.

Most states do not require pre-filing of this form before you raise capital in their state. Your legal adviser can tell you what filing is required. Filing fees are small and you can typically offer your program to investors right away.

Don't be fearful of using the Free Enterprise System to build up your business and increase your wealth and prosperity. Don't be fearful of accelerating ideas to reach markets. If you are not the CEO of your own ideas, have your ideas placed with a CEO who includes you as full partner to the process. Use the lessons you have learned about fear and taking new action to go all the way. Avoid delay and procrastination to bring new ideas to the rest of us. Rush new ideas to all the rest of us. And remember, your Golden Circle is working by your side. You are not doing this work alone! Super Achievers surround themselves with Golden Circles to develop ideas into global services.

Have an attorney **review** your document for $1,500 instead of creating it for $25,000. Make sense for the new capital demands of the Super Achiever Mindset?

If you are not good at preparing capital documents, obtain a member of your mastermind team who CAN and WILL complete the forms in record time. Suggest ten days at the most, from start to finish, and obtain clear written agreements as to what the teammate receives and the arrangement on the critical performance of time.

TIP: On all time agreements – make sure they are expressed in writing or consider you have no agreement at all. Include language in time agreements that detail check periods to see if a percent of the work is complete and always on a SHOW-ME basis. Don't wait until the end of the timeline to check. Super Achiever Mindsets hold performance accountable in every aspect of relationships with fewer exceptions than those who fail to hold the SA mindset.

Ok. Now, you are ready to begin.

So what happens now?

UNLIMITED CAPITAL IS A STATE OF MIND

Because I am not an attorney, I cannot provide specific legal information or advice. You must take action only with professional, licensed legal advice before you proceed. The information contained in *Super Achiever Mindsets* on capital formation expresses the author's personal opinion about the state of things at the time this publication was written. Seek out the best legal advice. Be honest, in all undertakings.

If you seek to change the world – to some degree you experience pain and suffering on elevated levels. Most of the time, our system works pretty well. Sometimes it fails. It is possible to do better and every lawyer and all judges know it. Hopefully, we'll do better.

Super Achievers have greater tests than those who fail to work on their mind state. You pass your tests by accepting every lesson – including betrayal, deception and unfairness with a heart that is unconditionally blame free and filled with forgiveness toward those who "know not what they do."

Never allow the lessons of life to deflect your focus.

TEN-DAY LIFE SUCCESS PLAN

Each reader is advised, you MUST obtain legal advice from licensed professionals before you undertake action on capital formation planning. The larger the enterprise the more specialized law firms of size and stature make sense. Keep in mind large law firms did not protect Arthur Anderson or Merrill Lynch from serious legal accountability in the early 2000s. Did these firms deserve the treatment they received – following years of public good and service? Many of the grandfathers of the investment industry think not. Who checks regulatory agencies when they run into political foul? The answer is – "we the people" do. The pendulum of injustice also swings back – and often the waste and greed of government is tempered by reformation or even revolution. Typically, the problem occurs when old software (systems) are applied to new future markets and a failure to upgrade the system lingers – making the system and its application obsolete. Compromise is required when Arthur Anderson or Merrill Lynch level players run into obsolete regulatory systems designed for ancient times before the modern problems occurred. Abuse, waste and misplaced blame often result from such antique systems. Eventually, the entire process upgrades. The markets insist upon it. The people of the Global Village are so awake today they recognize the abuse for what it is and the popularity of those in public service fails to shine as brightly as it will – when the upgrades are matured. The upgrades are coming. It is an exciting time to be alive.

However, remember the information you receive on legal compliance will vary, the price will vary as well from firm to firm. If you've ever shopped for tomatoes, you make certain you look over a few fresh products before you buy. Turn them over, make certain they are fresh and there is no hidden spoilage (costs) in the quote. Some lawyers will work on the promise of later payment which is ideal. Shop for partners who will work on your team. Someone on your team has a lawyer that is a brother, uncle etc. Find the right combination.

Shop and save is the rule not the exception for legal advice. New ideas and divisions should pay as little as possible in all fees until the idea is launched.

1. Form two or three NETWORKING TEAMS of five to seven individuals. Avoid family and friends. Choose team members who see you as an expert in your own idea. Choose a team who adds resume value and competency to your entire team work.

2. Three teams provide 21 potential capital assistants helping you complete capital funding in ten days or less. Team meetings may occur in a circle of chairs, at your home, with coffee and pastries. Team members for these network projects are not creating ideas as a mastermind team. Network teams are working as referral helpers; to introduce your ideas to highly "pre" qualified investors who might wish to participate in such an opportunity. Remember, however, only your core team, as authorized officers and directors of the company, has the legal right to offer securities to capital providers.

3. Tell each team about your new idea, and about HOW you are planning to raise capital. Use a white board or a PowerPoint presentation.

4. Ask each team member to be responsible to help you obtain a MINIMUM of THREE capital individuals who have the inclination and the immediate capital to invest $30,000 or more into your idea, within ten days, at a breakfast or lunch meeting you and your team plan – so all your meals are now FULL of qualified capital providers. Remember, 21 people – 7 in each of 3 teams – are now working to bring 3 or 63 individual investors into your orbit. They won't all say yes. They won't all do what they promise. So you will, through the Ten-Day Capital plan, still have enough new qualified investor connections. Super Achiever results happen fast – in ten days or less. The key is your mindset and your team organization. CEOs at any level can plan a start date and begin to maximize meal meetings with pre developed capital providers at your level of play. Never delay new ideas reaching the market.

5. Explain the deal in clear compelling terms. Use a "deal sheet" from your magic folder that explains the detail from the investor point of view.

6. Explain the urgency of building shareholder value through the profit centers you next explain as risk reducers.

7. Explain the risk of losing all the capital against the reward of the earnings multiple that can also be realized. Ask for a decision to invest and complete the documentation at the time the presentation is made. Always determine the next step to secure the

investment if any delay from your meal meeting occurs. Learn the sequence for each investor's decision process and check-list through each procedure.

You don't have to be an expert in this area. You don't have to like this work. You only have to do this work once, and your new Super Achiever life with Capitalism has begun. Every budding Super Achiever can master the Capital skill of our global Free Enterprise System. The objective is to rush ideas to benefit all the rest of us into manifestation. Super Achievers are master Manifestors.

We can only introduce model concepts here, and this information must be seen as introductory. You will require expert advice to proceed to obtain rapid funding documents. Your tour of www.SEC.GOV will provide the complete and most current rules relevant to your level of capital requirement. Everyone reading this book is only TEN DAYS away from new funding for your Super Achiever ideas. All that is required is for Super Achievers to compress the time to ACT on the information you are now studying.

There are live classes on Free Enterprise Skill that will help complete your education (including MBA refresher – upgrading classes) all of which help make CEOs huge immediate winners in the game of upgrading mental software first.

Dr. Mark Victor Hansen, top trainer for such companies as Century 21 Real Estate, Equitable Life Insurance and many others (also founding co author of the *Chicken Soup for the Soul* book series) produces a wonderful class on multiple sources of income and capital creation with Bob Allen of No Money Down Real Estate – drawing upon our own IBI principles. It is well worth the effort to fly to Dr. Hansen's next class on Multiple Sources of Income. (800 433-2314)

Jack Canfield hosts wonderful classes on self-esteem. Jack's trainings help individuals gain the self confidence to go out and do it, without every falling back into old habits. CEO-grade advanced classes for entire leadership teams can be reserved by the foremost trainer in the world on the topic. (800 237-8336)

Joel Roberts, David Fowler, Larry Ransom (corporate trainers for newspaper and electronic media – Wal- Mart and Target store management teams – and Microsoft and Hallmark Cards) and up to 30 other leading Fortune 500 Instructors join me in hosting the most advanced training in this field ($6,500 lifetime CEO membership) known as the FREE ENTERPRISE FORUM. You can obtain information about these classes by calling 256 774 5444 or click www.ibiglobal.com to watch videos online.

Leading companies are now investing larger budgets to reward team leaders as the asset of tenure is more recognized by corporate executives. Jane Willhite's PSI trainings provide the most important personal growth trainings available perfected over thirty years. (707 998-2222)

Professional firms such as McKenzie and others offer on site trainings over a wide range of software upgrades. Seek our Super Achiever mindset training and ask your training teams what is offered on this master skill set of mind.

Team reformation begins inside the mind. Group training to define new upgrades for the mind refine team output as team leaders are rewarded. The IBI Global program is the only formal team leader management training inclusive of the entire family at all ages, a trend now being carefully studied.

REFORM YOUR TEAM THINKING – REFORM YOUR RESULTS

FINANCIAL IMPERATIVES

Every man and every woman reading this book must consider certain real world information to direct his/her future. Your way of life will soon alter in ways you thought were impossible. To build financial freedom in today's world new skills are required. It is no longer OK to sit in one job for life and rely on your retirement for security. If you love your work, develop multiple income sources that are NOT jobs, as you fully partner with helping others.

Success is developed on a Super Achiever Mindset of INCREASE. The idea behind the mental software upgrade of INCREASE as a rightful living state – is the notion that your life exists to more broadly help others. As you apply new knowledge to more highly organize your time – you can do far more in less time. Your freedom expands rather than shrinks. Increase-minded men and women live the lives of greater freedom.

Success freedom includes success in spirit, success in relationships and joy filled lives that permit full exploration of the natural wonders of our environment. Total Success is a consequence of living in the Super Achiever Mindset.

Every author likes to preach a bit. As I age into oblivion, my global work to help finance bygone ages of infrastructure all over the world – an ode to three decades of antique services providing grease to the Global Village through development…in recent times, my mission (and I hope my legacy) revolves around Super Teaching, an invention for education. By providing accelerations for human learning the potential within every child can become a full partnership to the Super Achiever Mindset. **Hopefully, education will embrace the interface to live human learners in a manner that is rewarding versus punishing to the hard wiring of the super learners entering this new age of discovery**. Old model classrooms no longer work – where Super Teaching classrooms do work.

In 2003, I remember when CBS in Texas asked me to speak – on the prime-time drive hour produced by Carl Whitlesea in San Antonio, Texas. I was speaking against Warren Buffet's prediction of a global financial meltdown due to World Bank insolvency from high risk derivative trading. I was asked to provide an opposing view – from the vantage point of investment banking – and my multiple prior correct financial predictions since 1999.

As the Dow sat sinking at 7200 – and the war in Iraq was opening in the following week – I joined the show to predict the Global Village had entered a new extended boom time. I reported, in my opinion, the boom would not abate until 2010 to 2012 when demographics, due to retirement and aging, shake the markets to a stop.

We suggested listeners phone their brokers. We noted we felt bonds would crash while equities of all categories would soar. By year end 2003, the markets had risen over three trillion dollars since that on-air radio prediction. In 2004 and 2005 we continue our optimistic view of the Global Village in the short term – always from a CEO perspective to plan and grasp opportunity. We were calling all Super Achievers.

In the long term, however our view is far different. Still, there are opportunities in the long term view as well. Increasingly, we report for news channels on financial issues – from a platform of investment banking and an uncommon network of CEOs and law firms we work beside. Our record on prediction has provided more home runs for the stations involved to a point audiences now ask when we will be "on air" – with pen in hand.

Our contrary views and opinions will not be popular – and yet, historically, our record of prediction is so accurate more and more CEOs are relying upon them for future planning.

We present some of the long term views here – for reference to future long term planning by Super Achievers thinking into the future – say ten years or more.

It is a growing opinion that every bank savings account, every retirement plan both public and private, every investment dollar in paper investments media including stocks, bonds, mutual funds, and the like, are doomed to be devalued to near zero. Most of your investments and accumulated wealth – long term – outside real estate – are scheduled for bust – at some unknown future date. Why?

The reason centers on global public debt led by the USA. We owe about 15 trillion dollars when you consider the guarantees outstanding for banks, insurance firms, social security and the like. We owe almost 10 trillion dollars as a "reported" public debt when this book was written, but it is going up so fast. The largest national outflow is the interest payment upon debt. "We the people" are living in an ocean of virtual debt unlike any prior time in history. Japan owes approximately 13 trillion in bad debts that will never be repaid to the banks – which must, in the end, transfer this staggering abuse to the public. There is, of course, no recovery for such sums – outside the following formulas – all of which are historic in nature – repeating history from Greece to Rome to modern day Paris or Washington D.C.

If I took a banded stack of thousand dollar bills and set it upon a table, you would only have one stack, inches high, to reach one million dollars before we saw the top of even one minute of the debt payments required to operate the business you know as "We the People." We, the people, not only don't have enough money to retire this massive debt; we, the people, do not earn enough in our lifetimes to retire the national debt. This problem is global and growing more serious as we age.

By 2050, the European aging problem will be so serious that the only two major economies dominating the planet will be China and the Americas by virtue of population demographics.

If I went on to one BILLION dollars – stacking it in hefty thousand dollar bills you would need a few rulers to measure this stack of one thousand dollars bills representing one BILLION dollars in U.S. greenbacks from your view point.

If I went on to show ONE trillion of the many trillions we the people now owe, the stack would rise some 63 miles into outer space. Now that's only for "one" TRILLION dollars. Multiply that number by thirty times between Tokyo and the United States and think how many miles out into space that pile of public debt warp drives into. Now, add in all the bad debts of nations – all the unpaid debt or unpayable debts of companies still held on bank books as good loans – and you begin to see even a starship is unlikely to stay ahead of the debt piling up – because all of the debt requires interest be paid to privately owned banks. What a concept.

At one time the "people" printed their own money. National wealth rose on such integrity. Today private banks contracted by governments print and control the people's money for a fee. The entire concept holds capitalism from its most enlightened future form. However, the better software of future "enlightened Capitalism" remains unstoppable. It may take a few more well-educated Super Achiever generations to get to this better future –

but via reformation or revolution the future is coming. Central bankers had better get ready for their own retirement as a truly Global Village money management system unfolds – a system we, the people, directly manage. We no longer need them, and we never could afford them. Central Bankers – the internet age has arrived and you are now redundant to social good. Again, in the opinion of a growing number.

Another example. Let's say you and I went in and started a business at the time of the Great Crusades, say around 300 AD. We were pretty bad businessmen and women, not a Super Achiever Mindset among us. We worked harder than today. In fact, we worked 365 days a year. We NEVER took even one day off.

No holidays. No vacations. Nothing. Just work. Fifteen hours each and every day. We knew that "early to rise and early to bed make a person healthy, wealthy....and dead" but we didn't care. We just kept doing it. For hundreds of years.

We lost ONE MILLION DOLLARS a day, and we lost this money year in and year out from the time of the Great Crusades until today.

Now consider: you would still have to lose ONE MILLION DOLLARS a day, for <u>another</u> ONE THOUSAND years, to equal one trillion dollars!

And, we owe lots of trillions of dollars, and the amount is growing and growing as you read. The ticker is rising at a rate – that is beyond public good. It doesn't take a Super Achiever to figure out the math.

In 1985 we might have manufactured a solution in real terms to this mess. By 1993 it would have required cutting Federal Spending over 50% and taxing every adult and corporate tax payer by 150% for the remainder of three generations into the future to begin to control the interest and principle payments.

Still, we would lose money until the year 2950, when we might, only MIGHT break EVEN. And, of course, no politician is ever going to take "those" real numbers into his home community. Too many bad-debt nations – too many corporate bad loans (Enron, WorldCom and many more) – too many late plans for Social Security – too many delays – too few Super Achiever Mindsets when it really counted.

If we keep on going the way we are traveling (and we can't really do anything else) our economy cannot pay its debt bills by the year 2050 to 2060. We are completely bust by 2075. Some say much sooner – but war seems to always lead us into the future so who knows? If old programs apply without new mental software upgrading – who knows? It is important for your new ideas to be blended in now – versus waiting – "your" new fresh ideas matter. Somewhere, some reader has solutions to these dire financial problems. Your Golden Circle and your teams may lead us into a non-war solution. A peaceful solution. A true resolution. The answer is one idea away. And millions of human lives may be actually saved – perhaps a financial global summit – a four-year serious solution summit – might be initiated to globally work out the problem. A single global plan – rather than the political spin management of local politics? It's an idea.

There are three choices when a government has spent more than the entire tax base of its people can support and pay off:
1. Drastically cut government services and spending while raising taxes to historically destabilizing levels.
2. Decide to not pay on public debt, going back on promises made by the government.
3. Inflate the economy by printing money, and pay the debt off later with increasingly worthless money.

In the history of the world, over 6,000 years, from Rome to

Lincoln, the decision has always been to INFLATE the money supply. 100% of the nations in our position choose this route. Why would history be different now?

The world is in the same boat today. Following the Iraq war – at a time nations like Brazil went off the grid and bank contagion (melt down) was spreading in 2001 and 2002 – Europe, Asia and the United States – fearing chaos and global melt down – initiated the largest reinflation of modern times. The reinflation globally is continuing, and the inflation times ahead appear to be quite dramatic.

Where once we feared deflation (the ultimate depression breeder reactor) we now learn to live with moderate inflation for perhaps a generation or even two.

How will you survive in the coming inflation? How will you survive knowing social security, pension funds, your home, your job, offer no real secure value even as prices rise and rise and rise? Eventually, the debts will be declared null and void, redefined, reset, rescheduled, and only the degree of the rescheduling remains in question.

The future, the financial result of restated debt is a FRESH START (a positive outcome) which means real savings and wealth is wiped out, and everyone starts over Together. How bad is that? For millions it will tie to their image of self and the power THINGS have upon them. They have not trained their mind inventory to be liberated and free. For some, it will mean not having enough to eat or access to health care. For others, it will mean restructuring, retraining and an entirely new life. We live in a fragile end time of a great post war economy – now stretched to its breaking point – via improperly distributed credit and debt.

The cornerstone question is "how long" can the global debt economy hold together before a Debt Holiday is declared as a universal resolution? Will the good times (inflation times) continue for say ten to twenty more years?...or for one hundred or even two hundred years? A growing group of experts predict that population shifts will create a 2050 to 2075 melt down – impossible to avoid.

One of the contraction periods is likely to be too severe – as the debt issues become "unmanageable" for the Central Banks of the leading economies. In the past, the depression cycles were more or less understood. The banks reorganized and government spending led the way out – typically, via war.

While the present cost of the war on terror is at 4% and growing, still it's nothing like the 24% of GNP for the Vietnam War, or the 42% of GNP for the World Wars.

Yet there are signs. Today, new industries such as "cruise ship debt" have passed a trillion dollars and continue to grow at almost 200 million per super ship. If a contraction forced major repossession of bad loans on failed cruise ship companies – what would the banks do? There is no demand for the cruise ship in a global depression – and without massive investment and crews the ships rot quickly. There are many similar "new" industry sectors that are debt driven and which fail to demonstrate a solution in a serious deflation spiral. All depressions result from serious deflation spirals as demand for everything contracts continuously.

The modern high tech interconnected world has yet to live through a major global financial contraction. All living things breathe. The cycle of all life including financial life is to expand followed by a time to contract. All economies experience historic depression. No economy has ever increased and increased and increased.

There are wild cards. Terror is a wild card. A 2003 Moslem conference in Malaysia opened with the stark speech by predicting for 2004 and 2005 that several hundred million Moslems would never be defeated by only three million Jews. Terror remains a financial wild card.

Longevity. Should central governments reverse aging and extend life via new genetic or technology breakthroughs, the financial rebirth to the present debt economy would be hopeful. The continued aging of the primary population work forces in Europe, the Americas and Asia promise a very bleak debt day of settlement as time marches on. Of course, all this is not happening to Super Achievers today. Today, the Debt Economy holds near term opportunity for vast riches.

You now have planning information you already knew at some level. There is always opportunity in foreknowledge.

If you were traveling to the moon at the speed of the Apollo team – and you continued to travel for your lifetime – the speed of the debt growing along side of you would remain far out front when principle and interest were considered together. You could not outrun the money debt piling up by your spaceship going at the speed of the Apollo crew – globally speaking. This vision provides a lot of zeroes behind an entry when three-fourths of the world are so poor and many are starving to death – unproductive – never to know full partnership in a debt economy driven by rules largely formed before the computer existed. Bringing the third world nations online into full partnership for the economies of the world is another wild card filled with options.

Is the idea of secondary income (Multiple Income Tasking) starting to make even more sense?

Consider: the Federal Government collects social security taxes every week. The money is then deposited into the Social Security Fund, which pays its CURRENT weekly obligation for its own bills. All that money...just to pay a single week of operation for the government – which borrows the funds from "your" social security general fund and trust funds. The remainder (a reported surplus held in trust for "us") is instantly LOANED back to the government to pay off the national debt. The Social Security Fund, week after week, accumulates "markers" from the Federal Government. Social Security reports to us, the tax payer, that the fund is IN SURPLUS. All IOUs (weekly Government Markers) are reported as a current, rock solid ASSETS. In effect, there is NO REAL MONEY in social security for the future – just U.S. debt loads ever growing – while "we the people" undertake to maintain a virtual bankrupt credit corrupted system – placing the ultimate consequence for the decisions we postpone now – on to our children and upon their children. It seems like such a bad idea. If you operated the ENRON-level reporting system the United States Government operates – with zero outside auditing or accountability – you would be placed into prison for fraud. The transgression would not have been without malice or forethought and the violations would have been long standing and repetitive. While we yearn for new leaders to provide outside real world audits to govern social security trust funds – and all U.S. income and outgo – the chance of such outside real world standards applying in the bankrupt debt economy is remote.

Why? The answer is one word – "panic." The leaders who know the real condition of the financial balance sheet inherited an ongoing shell game. No one wants to tell the people what is under the real world shell. Our leaders are afraid of panic that will once and forever deflate the debt balloon – end shell game.

One wild card is panic, or runs on banks – when confidence finally shatters as the truth leaks out. A growing number of smart planners are holding their core assets in gold, silver and metals. Paper money "IS" the shell game and as a tool perpetuating the debt economy – may not be the ideal place to store future wealth. A great leader will come. They always do (historically speaking) and a FRESH START will begin. Hopefully, this time – the lessons of the past might be learned without war and global bloodshed.

Another wild card is manmade mass destruction via accident from biological or technological (nano technologies) development. One leading scientific authority in 2003 predicted the level of a worldwide disaster from man made tampering in 1974 had risen to 24% given all the new tools at mankind's disposal. In 2004 the estimate rises to just over 50%. End game.

Financial ignorance and political spin control are now ripping our potential Free Enterprise legacy into pieces. In such a climate, it's no wonder an outsider "Arnold the Movie Actor" becomes Governor of the richest and most debt-ridden state in the nation. In 2003, the historic recall simply indicated "we the people" were mad as hell and we wanted an outsider to take control versus more politics of deception and compromise.

Political change in 2005 through 2010 promise the most racially-shifted, gender-shifted political landscape in recorded history. Demographics show us growing a leading Hispanic population in the United States – as one nation – followed by Asian voters, followed by blacks, with whites becoming out-voted and out-numbered.

The 2005 to 2012 period will represent the most extreme pressure period for the debt economy central bankers. The wild cards being played – the need to avoid panic when the social security systems of all nations are, in fact, bankrupt – and when no solutions are showing themselves – produce unmanageable pressure. The Central Bankers have no solution. The system they invented for us is flawed – by profit and greed – always presented with the best intentions. Six million Jews were killed with the best intentions. Racial cleansing whether in Africa, Bosnia or Russia always presents the idea with the best intentions in mind – for those making the presentation. The money Nazis of the present debt economy will one day pass into memory...another well meaning idea that failed in fact to deliver superior results to the people of the world.

How could Central Bankers justify the interest they charge to "we the people" they serve? How could their system which precludes billions from even playing in the game – living lives without education or sanitation – starving while we pay farmers to NOT GROW FOOD – become a policy – regardless of how well intended? Any Super Achiever could suggest it was not "for the common good."

Revolutions are fought over taking control from Central Bankers. Perhaps, Super Achievers welcome a reformation or revolution every one hundred years or so. Revolutions represent the idea high bandwidth from the source – transmitted in bursts – wirelessly – at a time everyone is ready to receive the message. Hold a Super Achiever mindset for the news you read. Read between the lines of the spoon-fed incoming and read online news from other nations to gain perspective on point. Travel. Get to know the conditions of the world. Super Achievers invest in being informed. Super Achievers make their own decisions – often against the commonly held view – to their own gain and security in most cases.

In fact, each weekly U.S. Debt marker to the social security TRUST FUND (hundreds of millions) is an unfunded future liability upon future generations. Week-to-week the saddle our grandchildren will carry gets heavier. The U.S. markers are secured by no plan of payment, no allocation from future resources, no contingent plan for payment and no assets to serve as security for the bogus off balance Enron-type loan scheme. Every year there are more workers retiring making claims on social security and fewer workers paying into social security.

Insurance that has more claims than premium payments –

goes bankrupt rapidly. The retiree lives longer – far more active lives. Social security has no plan or asset base to meet its promises. We all know it. We just lack the details. We did not know the government was borrowing from the Trust Fund to meet current obligations with annual budget deficits in all but a few of the fifty years of post war history.

Meanwhile, the interest on the debt is almost at the point when 150% of tax payer income would still not pay the debt obligations for even ONE YEAR. Older Americans and the AARP are increasingly working on "real resolutions" against the politics as usual. In the end, we the people – armed with accurate truthful facts – no matter how unpleasant - will make the hard choices. The world is ready for a reformation if not a revolution. A peaceful global village is the desired outcome.

Today, the interest on the national debt is as large an item as Social Security for the entire nation, or Defense! 75% of the entire annual budget is contained in almost equal wedges of Social Security, Defense and INTEREST. The rest of the pie is the more than 11,000 other Government programs, fighting for 25% of the remaining dollars. And this pie wedge is SHRINKING, while the debt load is growing. No wonder our largest growing cities are prison. No wonder social services are now being terminated in record numbers. No wonder the people are electing movie actors to the top jobs – so little hope remains and so much frustration exists.

Meanwhile, CEOs at the top fail to band together into their own Super Achiever Clubs to assure the "right idea" reaches the right markets.

ONE IDEA AND THE RESOLUTION BECOMES CLEAR

Tricky, almost magical, accounting technology (not permitted for non government entities) makes the public debt look much smaller than it is. The government does every day what Enron always feared to do. The potential for fraud on the American People is so staggering that only a real independent audit by OUTSIDE audit firms (some wish it were Arthur Anderson as lead audit controller) –could uncover the true accounting scandal. When all public guarantees are considered the public obligation is more like 15 TRILLION DOLLARS today and growing at a rate unseen in American history. Private bankers collect and PROFIT from the interest, not we the people – a small group of privileged invisible debt lords profit – a repeat of ancient history – at the hands of virtual serfs unable to rise up and revolt.

DEBT LORDS CONTROL THE FUTURE OF THE GLOBAL VILLAGE

We don't have enough money or assets in the Global Village to meet the Debt load – as every third world government so well knows. Looking to the United States – itself bankrupt on paper – for relief and never-ending new flows of capital – is unrealistic until the credit bubble finally bursts and self corrects. However, the DEBT LORDS using controlled inflation and regulated depressions (deep recession cycles) may avoid panic – and resolution to the Debt realities for many years into the future. Super Achievers must be awake to the core reality even while they deal with the near term markets. Plan accordingly. Hedge your plan and resources with better information. Plan for the worst and anticipate the best. For the time being, the world's DEBT LORDS have all the cards and hold all the power.

TIP: All Free Enterprise financial systems are self correcting over time regardless of the level of abuse heaped upon them.

The combined bridges, damns, highways and buildings of the Global Village do not make a dent in the growing debt and interest chains against the total combined earning power of the

Global Village. Remember what ONE TRILLION is - miles into outer space. We just can't earn as fast as the Debt Lords profit from our antique system of doing business. The core software is virus filled. We the people must one day remove the virus (systems) and replace the code with an upgrade that is virus free and which crashes hopefully – not at all. Rebooting (war) has become too painful – we need an operating system for the Global Village that works – all the time – without the need for rebooting. A better way is coming – the only question really – is when. As we've pointed out, historically speaking – these are the times which try men's (and women's) souls. They are also sensationally exciting times in which to bear witness to history, repeated or otherwise. A great adventure is unfolding, and we are all part of the ride.

Again, is your own secondary income (multiple source of income) representing new rivers of cash that YOU CONTROL, making even more sense to you? Super Achievers live multiple income life styles because they understand the simple economics of debt.

Controlling multiple rivers of cash flow in exchange for services is a security no one can take away from you. In the future, real security may depend upon capital holders taking their funds away from traditional plans and putting their money into VENTURE INVESTING (to underwrite new cash flow sources). Real security may require Multiple Income Tasking for each Super Achiever individually as well as corporately. Super Achiever Business owners will wish to assure that each business has multiple income "feeders" to the core business – as a plan of future business undertaking. Super Achievers make better plans in all markets. Plan defensively – plan more wisely – plan with better information. Super Achievers help one another in the planning process – as an attribute of the Super Achiever mindset.

Financial survival may depend on a greater NUMBER of business or personal income sources you create in your life. Having at least THREE is ideal for the average Super Achiever business model or individual income plan.

However, you may be caught in the punishment syndrome of thinking money must be earned from a J.O.B alone (sometimes defined as…Just Over Broke – Journey Of the Broke – or another JOB without Multiple Income Planning inside). Are you locked into a one-source income approach to your life plan? Regardless of how strong your multi million dollar JOB may be at the moment – you are well advised to review your own Multiple Income Technology plan – while time is on your side.

What's wrong with such a plan from a Super Achiever Increase lifestyle perspective?

How does the single JOB approach to life maximize your contribution to all the rest of us? Does a multiple income approach leverage your capacity to benefit even more of us?

If it fails to address the issue of "how does your plan" regularly increase value to all the rest of us – rethink your plan. Secure team help. Better plans create better income. Better plans create more secure income. Increase (in social contribution throughout an entire life spectrum) is a Super Achiever mindset. Super Achievers never retire from social contribution during the course of their lives. Mature Super Achievers (65 in age and older) tend to direct more than implement operational aspects of contribution. Super Achievers naturally move from operational activity to director level activity as maturity grows and wisdom rules.

CEOs should all earn CASH FLOW RIVERS from various sources as a mark of "increase" in social contribution. For example, can you sit on two or three Network Teams (boards) and consult to more than one area of interest in your life – always increasing income as a natural way of life - when the projects are controlled and operated by others? CEO-to-CEO networking becomes the master environment for the Super Achiever lifestyle of Increase. Super Achievers discuss and synergistically support increase as a lifestyle. Bob Harrison's work on Increase as a lifestyle via Bob Harrison Seminars online is a worthy investment in books and tapes for the aspiring Super Achiever.

Increase applies to your mental software. If you earn a million or more today – associate with others who also earn at this level while remaining committed to increase as a lifestyle. Remember to bring up another "you" each year who in the future will reach your level of earnings (service to society) and surpass this level of earnings – keeping in mind competition systems are being replaced by cooperative systems in all forms of organization. If you fail to mentor other "copy cats" to your station of success (social contribution) you fail to own the Super Achiever Mindset. Super Achievers are all Master Mentors.

MASTER MENTORS CONTRIBUTE MORE TO THE GLOBAL VILLAGE

Can you publish a book and earn some royalties from your story? Will your book feed your core business? How fast can we develop capital and complete that work? Can we hire ghost writers to complete the book in six weeks now that we have capital? Is the idea to learn, earn and return your natural lifestyle, your dominant thought pattern? The dominant thoughts you hold in your mind manifest as your reality. Different realities represent different states of mind.

Can you find a game or invention and broker the game or invention to make some new royalties while millions are better entertained or educated?

Can you create an idea for a service or product and form a Team that will start the business and DO the business, while you work on your primary job and serve as a director in the venture relationship?

Free Enterprise Skills are empowering and freeing. Financial Freedom is a ratio to the Free Enterprise Skill you discover in life. Couples are strengthened by working to develop new Free Enterprise Skills together.

Super Achiever Mindsets is an ideal publication for life partners to study together. Share the experience of reforming your Decision PROCESS. Elevate your thinking together. Plan new Super Achiever Association in your teams for the coming months. INCREASE becomes a state of mind that with proper like minded association becomes "the" habitual prime operating system – the one you use and rely upon.

Everyone uses time to better advantage when Free Enterprise Skills are employed for the benefit of others. The ultimate FAMILY GAME in the 1990 is FREE ENTERPRISE AMERICA with "cooperation systems" inside. A winning score shows up as IN-COME beside elevated output and performance for all levels of endeavor.

Early success will allow you to live a debt free lifestyle, the best lifestyle for the inflation time that is inevitable ahead. Super Achievers monitor global markets for deflationary spirals – that breed depression economic contraction and the contagion that often leads to panic. Planning for the best with a defensive posture always preparing for the adjustment maintains a safe port in the financial storms that ravage the Debt Econo-seas.

Pay your home off. Your key security asset will be your home or your many homes all debt free. Invest in real property. If a crash occurs, real property will plummet in value – but all things are relative. Your debt-free properties will remain value-based in any economic model. Many experts may tell you not to do it....our opinion – do not listen to them. History is a superior teacher. Invest in income property that is likely to survive a crash. It may not happen in your lifetime. If inflation economies continue – your generation will make a fortune. If a crash comes, invest in basic rental properties for residence – for base services from hair cuts to health care as lease tenants.

Another note – on security – Life Insurance money managers represent virtually the only "professional money managers" to never miss a payment – even when the banks closed from panics. Life insurance investing ranges from annuities to whole life permanent life insurance – avoiding variable policies that invest in the market – as another safe port in the storm. Life Insurance investing is as "safe as gold" for Super Achiever mindsets. Super Achievers are over insured for a reason.

In the present economy, tax law favors business life insurance investing. Moving more resources into life insurance products may be a sound hedge plan long term – offsetting the risks of the Debt Economy. Keep in mind, we do not know the time when the Debt Lords will lose their influence to hide behind the spin control and debt controlled media culture. In the end, the media will turn on its debt hosts as if they were parasites, and the truth, once again, will set us all free. Super Achievers monitor conditions with superior information when they lay down plans, always keeping the "possible" futures in mind.

Another wild card – is the one of how FAST the market can reform from competitive (debt managed) economic systems into cooperative new models for enlightened capital. Electronic, real-time trading – improved real-time regulation – and replacement of central bank systems in favor of TEASURY direct systems unified into a single world power currency – all represent wild cards for future prosperity. Sustainable prosperity is possible with the modern global tools available – but only within a cooperative, not competitive global plan versus a region-to-region, slug-it-out dynamic. Economically speaking, a one-world everything is the only future for humanity. From rain forest economics (breathing) to distribution economics (instant communications) cooperation promises great progress – however – we do not know the speed by which competitive systems will reform into cooperative systems. The process initiated in the 1970s to reform virtually all Global Systems along these lines – favored by both Dr. Edward Deming and my father, Alan G. Dohrmann, has become – already in this short span of several decades – unstoppable. Super Achievers work together to increase the Velocity Acceleration and Momentum (VAM) of the system's transformations.

In all markets, we suggest leaders apply their secondary multiple income streams to pay down debt as the first priority of future security. Become free of the Debt Lords and your future freedom becomes more secure. Pay off your homes and your investment properties and your personal consumer goods. Leverage in moderation on very short term plans for future accumulations. Super Achievers lead debt free lives. Eliminate debt from your life and maximize income into your life plan. As you apply age-old biblical principles to your life and the life of your grandchildren, you create a global village that is more empowered to assist one another in cooperation economics.

Invest in new Free Enterprise Venture opportunities – fueling the future with your time, your ideas and your resources including your connections. Help one another cooperatively. My new publication *Redemption* is a systems guide for Super Achievers who wish to move forward into a future of cooperative thinking. Our hope remains that *Redemption* will become a legacy "bible" for methods and sequence to repair competition virus code on the mental computer of the reader – with new better code based on cooperation. New systems for thinking reformation have been laid out in *Redemption* to assist Super Achievers with their mental upgrade process. The future is always a matter of choice.

Choose activity that will thrive in the likely inflation times. Earn lots of income from MULTIPLE sources. Take surplus from your success and invest in the dreams others have. Create new wealth whenever possible. NEW wealth is the key to success for the future of our truly global society. Together we are creating a braver new world – a pure FRESH START...one Super Achiever at a time.

Assume greater personal responsibility for the performance of our nation, one Multiple Income Task at a time! Become active in politics. Every vote counts. Every idea counts. Place yours into the political system. Avoid apathy. Become active in politics as a Super Achiever Mindset. Give time and dollars to political reformation.

Master the principle of MULTIPLE SOURCES OF INCOME (MSI) in the months ahead and perfect the process over a lifetime. Your life is made more useful to all of us and you are paid accordingly.

Attend seminars and classes on these subjects and upgrade the software of your mind. Acquire the tools of Free Enterprise that permit the MSI lifestyle to thrive and lead others to join you in this style of freedom. MSIs work in every country, in every nation, in every village in the world. Learning the principles to create such opportunities can be accelerated by the United Nations and host countries. A Free Enterprise skill training opens the world to full partnership and cooperation. Look for books and tapes on these subjects and study skill enhancement material at least once a quarter. There are programs for beginners. There are programs for MBA CEOs at the top of the leading companies in the world. Frequent mental upgrading is the key to maintaining a fresh perspective in the accelerating options now being manifested everywhere. Old ways of thinking die hard. Test your own belief and borders by the "time" you invest annually in "retraining" your mind to think with a cleaner, fresher edge. Leaders at the top – challenge yourselves.

Corporate leaders, consider how you will map out strategy to prosper in the years to come, the years dominated by LIFESTYLES OF THE DEBTORS AND LENDERS – THE DEBT LORDS; Policy made by bond holders; Expansion made by market timing; Ownership opportunities via proxies. Key your core plans and undertakings to position within the new DEBT reality. The Debt Lords are working on failed software that has failed to stand the test of time – using competitive versus cooperative systems to manage economics. The new enlightened capital will simply pass them by in the coming age where enlightened capital leads humanity to a peaceful world and exploration to the stars.

How will the growing inflation affect your business practices in the near term? How will you react to local deflation spirals or the potentials for rapid contagion? Do you have a master plan "just in case" for both areas? If not – why not? Does it make sense to make developing such plans a priority? Can you create such "what if" plans without outside expert coaching?

Have you planned to win in the new international debt wars that are developing? These debt wars will position national interests, sovereign peoples and nations, one against the other for finite supply; finite claim on distribution; and finite claim on power. Power shifts made possible by the DEBT BOMB. Using Debt as a financial tool of state, of corporate power, or chess – not checkers – is the BIG THINKER'S way to the future in corporate global planning. The future belongs to the distribution SYSTEM. Today, China buys more of our national debt than any other nation. Japan is second. Consider the power of "who controls the debts of the United States of America?" Do you see this item featured in the news presented by the children of the Debt Lords? Those who finance the media do not report on their own secret state of the union. Super Achievers research the facts and draw their own conclusions.

Superior Distribution SYSTEMS will survive the changing climates. New corporate (collective awakening) for information management, more alert wakeful corporate decision-making and superior vision for the alignment of interests to future market conditions are required. These skills are waiting to be renewed and developed within the mature corporate culture.

My advice to leaders is the same advice I give one mind at time to individuals seeking SUPER ACHIEVER performance. Invest your tax dollars into education and retraining once a year – mental retraining is the core skill of the coming age. Retrain your mental conditioning to fine tune your performance on a year-to-year basis. In today's accelerated markets even two years is too long to refrain from retraining. Plan five and ten year mental development programs for your teams. Reward key leaders with a corporate rewards program.

In the past, you acquired EVENT technology. The teaching event started and then stopped. In the future, you will purchase PROCESS TECHNOLOGY training. Each new training program will be part of a process, one following the other that leads toward elevated measurable success in human performance gains. Productivity will soar. Creativity will accelerate. Profits will rise and remain predictable in changing times. These assets are impossible to maintain unless leaders retrain.

For everyone the mission is so obvious. You must DO SOMETHING about what you have been reading. Inactivity shuts the book, closes the information and leaves you no better than when you started. Retrain is a verb. The mind requires food to grow. Feed the mind short power bursts of retraining – to expand and refresh pools of collective thought in your organization. The plan to retrain works equally well for the professional, sole proprietor or Fortune team at the top.

Every day you CONSIDER doing something about your future is a day that could have been marked by your DECISION.

Simply....the choice has always been YOURS and YOURS alone to make!

If you think enough time has gone by already, *Super Achievers* becomes more than just another book you once read.

Super Achiever Mindsets becomes a way of life.

Is it time to make a decision?

REVIEW

We have discussed possible paths for economic condition far into the future. We have discussed solution planning. We have listed some key mindsets by which all Super Achievers:

- Seek out one another
- Cross mentor one another
- Invest time to mentor regularly at peer level
- Invest to retrain the mind
- Plan for the best; prepare for the worst
- Read the news with a different eye
- Adopt cooperation as a global reform movement
- Accelerate cooperation into systems at all levels
- Understand Debt Lord economic modeling
- Embrace enlightened capitalism and plan to be the model by example

- Invest in ventures
- Live debt free lifestyles
- Adopt INCREASE as the dominant thought to measure contribution to society
- Support cooperative resolutions to war solutions standing for world peace

MAY ALL FUTURE INCREASE AND POSSIBILITY BE YOURS

BALANCE is as important a super achievement as any executed idea. And each of you can have it all. All of you can be more and do more than you possibly imagine. This mindset holds true for Mr. and Mrs. Gates as it holds true for the leaders of the free world. The enterprises you work within and influence, or found and build, might open with charters that discuss the policy of employee rewards, balance, and the intangible things that permit teams to thrive together.

New Empires of the mind can be HAD.

Financial Freedom can be WON.

And with balance and the new security higher output provides, success becomes a more broad reality with cooperation increasingly replacing competition as a failed model for any human organization.

Balance is the lifestyle you alone can shape around your personal life.

Our objective is always to arrive at the learn, earn and return point we call PRIME. Prime is a state of Super Achieving that is sustained over a life time. Prime grows you as much as you grow and maintain the state of Prime. Prime can produce income of hundreds of thousands of dollars or hundreds of millions of dollars – while both ends of the income spectrum measure only – the degree by which your life has benefited others.

Prime is the single state Super Achievers aspire to reach.

Prime includes the following stages restated for the reader's later application:

Stage I – Prime – Investment income exceeds "earnings" by double

Stage II Prime – Balance – Super Achievers work Tuesday, Wednesday, and Thursday and cease working on other days – increasing time for charity and enjoyment of relationships, the planet and lifetime learning.

Stage III Prime – Charity – Charitable gifting increases for three consecutive years – providing sustainable prime – income is now seen as a means to increase charity – versus personal accumulation.

Super Achievers aspire to live their lives in a condition we call THE PRIME STATE. I ask that Super Achievers join me by working on MY global Life Success Team; that you commit to the Mission Statement my Team has adopted with 100% commitment and acceptance:

- To always challenge yourself to improve conditions of living the human experience.
- To express yourself in creative perfection by growing, developing and demonstrating new realities into your unfolding experience.
- To surround yourself with positive, uplifting support in every aspect of your life and to settle for nothing less. Perfect the process.
- To deny self-talk that includes blame, judgment or "why we can't" mental energy and to replace such programs with upgraded mental code.
- To move away from those who fail to support your highest and best good – leaving them fully magnificent without blame or judgment limiting

"those" you back away from – in life. Proceed with gentleness, kindness and charity.

- To seek pleasure, joy and bliss from the rewards of surrounding yourself with truly like minded supporters, enriching every hour of life.
- To aspire to Prime lifestyles – a Super Achiever birthright – ever increasing your contribution to all of the rest of us.
- To teach and instruct others how to find their Golden Circles and to elevate life to the Super Achiever Mindset. Invest part of your life as a Master Mentor.
- To seek and to never tire of higher fields of illumination for your unfolding adventure of mental program – upgrade your mental software with retraining – annually at least. Rise to razor sharp mental focus.
- To reward yourself with self love. You are fully deserving, entitled, worthy and created to enjoy the living experience with an abundance of infinite unlimited intelligence. Your mind can set you free.
* Adopt the mission of helping Super Teaching reach more schools worldwide. Adopt the mission to replace competitive models and systems in all human organized activity – as the more ideal model for future human endeavor. As you participate in the cooperative systemic change taking place in the Global Village you help usher in a new era of discovery for human kind.

TWILIGHT IN ALABAMA

I look back on the past fifty plus years and think how extraordinary they have been. Raised by a family of privilege in San Francisco's golden era, heir to a rich legacy of family traditions and history.

Alan Girard Dohrmann, a leader in shaping what is now the 100 BILLION dollar a year corporate training industry of the 1940's to the present, and the human potential educational industry – President and CEO of PSI World until he died. Father to nine of us, Dad practiced his training lessons upon his children first. Each of us have benefited from his "stories" over the term of our own lives.

I think of my teachers and include Penn Patrick and my father, Alan Dohrmann. I think of my friends and close associates – Barry Spilchuk and his *Cup of Soup* book; his *Let's Talk* work to save one million marriages - or Lisa Nichols with her soon-to-be-released *Chicken Soup for the African American Soul* – Eve Hogan with *Intellectual Foreplay* and *Chicken Soup for the Singles Soul* – I think of Jill Lublin and *Guerilla Public Relations* – or John Gray, author of *Men are from Mars* - and Dwight Chapin, President Nixon's appointment secretary in the White House. I cherish my mentorship by Raleigh Shaklee and George Witter of Dean Witter (now owned by Morgan Stanley); Rafi Brown in Israel; the late Harry Openhiemer in South Africa; the late, Tom

Willhite from California and my dear friend, Jane; the late, Val Van De Wall from Edmonton, Canada; Lee Pulos in Vancouver; and Mark Victor Hansen with Jack Canfield in Southern California; Wally Minto and a few others such as Art Lachman of San Francisco. Of course, there are so many new teachers coming into my life like David Fowler, as well as my legacy teachers such as Bob Harrison. I know I'm leaving many out and I ask everyone to consider that our work – is better because of you – each of you and all who follow you. We are so grateful for our teachers and I want to personally thank them all, those alive and passed – each and every one.

There are so many other extraordinary men and women who have taught me in my life - not to mention the elder George Bush and Peter Uberoth two of my great mentors. And my favorite from my early years, Alice Mahoney. And the most important, my wife Virginia Lynn Dohrmann – a leading woman out front on today's battlefield of challenge. All of my children have taught me so much – how could they not?

But perhaps my greatest lessons have been learned from the playing field of life itself – playing as a husband, corporate leader, father, inventor, author and teacher. As I sit by the Tennessee River, in a bend, lined with trees and tranquility much of the five decades of service and history (almost six decades as these words go to print) is gone from memory and the world. Lynn and I will talk it over with the family "babies" we are helping to raise and think about what their life will be like in some unknown future. We take long, lazy walks on a dead end "deliverance like" road - deep in the southern forests no would could find even with a GPS and a map – trust me.

In the fall colors or the spring bloom, grandma and grandpa hold hands in our "little life" and map out what comes next – perhaps with steps that come slower now – and reflections on the future that are even sweeter now – as even the smallest squeeze of our hands conveys oceans of memories across the fabric of our arms. Our hearts receive the message as one, as the long, slow breezes of the South pass us by. We easily imagine the next generation taking walks along this forgotten roadway never knowing we stopped frequently to see the waterfall or when we spotted a bright red Cardinal of particular magistracy – or a common deer – or perhaps an owl. Our lives are full of such important day-to-day events, and we hope our readers will follow these lazy bone walks often as they adopt their own Super Achiever mindsets.

We sometimes talk about the past, but not much really --

The fourteen countries we operated our offices within, our company brochures in seven languages, tens of thousands representing our companies and services, and thousands of employee jobs created - and through their efforts millions of other jobs created as the investment capital ebb and flow found its way into the new industries we helped finance. The private jets and related perks of the day. The things the mind can create and achieve. If you only believe it. Our memories of what we have shared, built, sold, moved on to, or labor to create today – all vibrations of mind – all transitory. We know the feelings so well. In the snapshot of life, we will graduate at the end days counting our blessings, numbering our like minded friendships – secure in the flowers we held in our hand – the mentorship we shared with others – and the mentorship we received – the owls and cardinals we stopped to gaze upon – along God's holy highway. Age has such privilege.

And, of course, I know so well that every reader, without exception can do far more than we thus far have been able to achieve; and do it multiple times; plus, enjoy doing it every day along the way, just as my Lynn and I have.

We are improving to balance life from my teaching work and my Super Teaching invention to include a bit more time for the birds and fall colors. I am learning "balance" with Lynn, my partner and very best friend, as my most important teacher about this state we call Prime. Perhaps it is truly unattainable alone – hence the desire to partner along the way. This tiny, little woman has provided more insight to how life should be lived than all my mentors, teachers and instructors combined. I think I'll continue to study her course material for the remainder of my days. There are always new lessons that surprise the worthy student.

I am asked wherever I lecture, "why do you reside in Alabama of all places – given the work is so globally important?" The accent the inquisitor places on Alabama becomes almost a degrading smirk universally applied.

I usually find the word "Alabama" to be stereotyped, belittling – when expressed. This attitude would not be present if I stated I was a fifth generation San Franciscan and gave the inquirer my blue blood linage.

I smirk back when I answer the inquirer about Alabama.

"I live in Ala-God-Bless-it-Bama for a lot of reasons, sonny!" I'm smiling now.

"I live in Alabama after all my research."

I usually pause here, until they ask me.

"What research?"

Well, let's look over God-Bless-it Al ah bama and see those vital statistics right where I live in Huntsville:

- 3% unemployment.
- Booming diversified economy
- Highest PHD per capita of any city in the country
- Highest engineering population per capita
- Highest income per capita in the 17 Southern

States – the Sunbelt move-in states
- Low prices for labor, housing, land, business support
- Superior tax rate
- Best climate in the Sunbelt
- Most friendly place to live on earth
- Family values second to none
- Home of the international space station and all future ideas for space exploration
- Home of more new technology than almost any other location on earth

I often ask the inquirer if they knew, "...why Area 51 was relocated to Huntsville, Alabama?" As they don't often know that this reality even occurred I tell them some of the items listed above.

They next ask "Why did the government relocate area 51 to Alabama?"

I inquire whether "they" can keep a secret.

They usually lean in and reply – "well, of course, I can."

I say – "Good – I'm happy I live in Alabama and we are the best at keeping a secret." And then I'm quiet. But we return to the research.

A lot of research really. Maybe it's the all new freeways with little traffic as our Huntsville lifestyle for 2010. The never-wait in any new place to dine, or movie theater. Meals feature selections from the Global Village usually reserved for New York or San Francisco. Maybe it's just the friendly down south lifestyle that is fading from every place in the world. Maybe it's the co-operation. Or just the concentration of so many mentors, coaches and Super Achievers all in one place, in one state, Alabama.

I suppose you can GET IT ALL somewhere else, but I don't

know where and I've had offices all over the world. The lifestyle in Alabama is SOOOO good I am afraid the rest of the world will discover it and begin to move in. So we discuss it very seldom. We love those smirks – we just go about our Southern way and let them return to their freeway rush hour traffic.

That a Gone-with-the-Wind home can be purchased for so little is a mystery to them.

And it's sunny and wonderful all the time – nor too hot and or humid. They just don't understand the research and we don't want to tell 'em.

But what about all that humidity? No, that's Florida. That's Houston. It's not HERE in northern AL-AHHHH-GOD BLESS IT BAMA!

I come home from speaking tours, or class instruction to a simple life with what Lynn and I refer to as "the little life" with our children and family. Alabama gives you TIME to enjoy the balance. I want it all to slow down for a bit, and Alabama still offers the quality – Alabama will SLOW YOU DOWN a few seconds after arriving. I am looking for like-minded, family valued, principled neighbors who say, "HI!" and really mean it! Eye contact is important in a super market or shopping mall. Alabama gives you eye contact you can feel friendly about.

To cease giving advice; to cease consulting; to cease teaching; and to share some real people values with real people, who are the nicest, most friendly society I have seen in the world today, these are MY decisions. I want my readers to know I am careful to live what I preach not just speak it. Alabama is a choice in life like everything else. In the end this San Francisco boy will be buried in the South beside his Southern Belle.

The reward for all the giving is a daughter too good to be true, a wife too wonderful and perfect to be compared, and a lifestyle every reader would envy.

So, what is the meaning of life?

The meaning of life is to fix your mind on dwelling about the future.

The meaning of life comes when you have the goals you desire, then SET BIGGER GOALS. File clerk your mind for perfection, and perfection will come!

And always, always think BIG. It costs nothing more to think really large wonderful thoughts. Don't settle for little dreams. Dream BIG. As you move along toward achieving your dreams – DREAM BIGGER DREAMS.

Life is a one-time ride. The adventure is your own adventure. Free Enterprise Skill is magic vehicle that will take you anywhere you desire inside the theme park of your own great life. Good things happen. Challenge happens. Your reaction is what sets you free. Hold your mind on your goal and always live to increase your service to all the rest of us. Allow yourself to become engaged in the how of doing this work with the core asset we call "your life."

Once you have your dreams growing, make certain you are living where you want to live, and living how you want to live. The old saying you ARE NOT A TREE is so true. Replant yourself until you discover your own sense of home.

You can move.

You can enjoy new experience.

The location you choose will dictate the type of mastermind team players you will have around you. You won't lose your old team. You will certainly meet a new team.

Financial Freedom is not worth having if you don't exercise it.

Alabama has also reinstated the conviction in my life that America hosts the most productive, inventive work force the world has ever seen. Our own future depends upon our abilities to generate second-to-none results in our day-to-day performance. Beginning with every individual.

As the twilight settles in Alabama, I think of the past number of years teaching Free Enterprise Forum classes to students from all over the world. Teaching small and large companies how to upgrade performance to levels once believed impossible.

I can see so many of their faces. From Korea. From Japan. From Europe. From Indonesia. From Australia, Canada and so many more. Men and women with dreams. Company managers with a burning desire to win the markets of the 21st century. All with a fervor to win. With some impossible ability to face their personal terrors and to walk through the eternal doorway of opportunity. I think of working with large charities and of founding our own. I think of the schools that now have Super Teaching inside because of our never-ending work to make it happen. I think of the graduates of our training programs now running exciting vibrant industries.

So many new businesses. New books. New music. New services. New inventions. New art. Ideas that once born became unstoppable.

Who can double and triple their personal income using multiple income technologies? The Answer is everyone can -

Judges can. Business owners making millions a year can. 21-year-old students can. Secretaries can. Doctors can. Homemakers can. Everyone can.

You should!

Super Achiever Mindsets is the decision reformation tool that breeds inspired performance from all of us in a marketplace of increasing cooperation.

My advice to the reader. Master the art of forming like minded power teams. Create your own new teams soon.

Meet on a regular basis and elevate your own performance

week-to-week.

Switch on your improved method for making a decision.

Wake up and never permit your thinking process to fall into lazy habits of lower awareness. You're too smart not to retrain your mind on a frequent basis. Invest the time and resources to make it happen.

From teaching these lessons to so many students I know one certainty. In some small or large way, lessons you have been exposed to in this book will remain yours for a lifetime.

When you face the never-ending flow of challenges in life, you may catch yourself reflecting to judge your state of mind against the Super Achiever mindset and smile.....and you remember the wonder and power inside your mind.

I wish you a simple prayer as we adjourn. For me, the end is a red ball of sunset that fills the twilight sky in Huntsville, Alabama, near the NASA Space and Rocket Museum.

For you, the end is my prayer for Mastermind Success Teams worldwide: that God grant you the most perfect possible future and the attraction to know the most perfect possible partners and companions to share this perfect future with.

May the abundance and prosperity of the Almighty Creator flow over and around the universe of those you love and seek to protect and always be present to guide you in your thoughts, to foster and keep you in the uncommon wisdom, to bring forth magnificence from you and in you for all you imagine in life, to make your journey ever more joyful in this life, a life of the Super Achiever existing as an eternal memory of perfection realized.....**AMEN!**

SUPER ACHIEVER APPENDIX

Please find following our research (this is a compilation from various authors) on the Federal Reserve Board Central Bank Authority - paid to manage the U.S. currency and debt loans - paying interest to itself.

Some people think the Federal Reserve Banks are United States Government institutions. They are not Government institutions, departments, or agencies. They are private credit monopolies which prey upon the people of the United States for the benefit of themselves and their foreign customers. Those 12 private credit monopolies were deceitfully placed upon this country by bankers who came here from Europe and who repaid us for our hospitality by undermining our American institutions.

The FED basically works like this: The government granted its power to create money to the FED banks. They create money, then loan it back to the government charging interest. The government levies income taxes to pay the interest on the debt. On this point, it's interesting to note that the Federal Reserve Act and the sixteenth amendment, which gave congress the power to collect income taxes, were both passed in 1913. The incredible power of the FED over the economy is universally admitted.

On June 4, 1963, a virtually unknown Presidential decree, Executive Order 11110, was signed with the authority to basically strip the Federal Reserve Bank of its power to loan money to the United States Federal Government at interest. With the stroke of a pen, President Kennedy declared that the privately owned Federal Reserve Bank would soon be out of business. The Christian Law Fellowship has exhaustively researched this matter through the Federal Register and Library of Congress. We can now safely conclude that this Executive Order has never been repealed, amended, or superceded by any subsequent Executive Order. In simple terms, it is still valid.

The Federal Reserve Bank, a.k.a Federal Reserve System, is a Private Corporation. Black's Law Dictionary defines the "Federal Reserve System" as: *"Network of twelve central banks to which most national banks belong and to which state chartered banks may belong. Membership rules require investment of stock and minimum reserves."* Privately-owned banks own the stock of the FED. This was explained in more detail in the case of Lewis v. United States, Federal Reporter, 2nd Series, Vol. 680, Pages 1239, 1241 (1982), where the court said: *"Each Federal Reserve Bank is a separate corporation owned by commercial banks in its region. The stock-holding commercial banks elect two thirds of each Bank's nine member board of directors"*.

The Federal Reserve Banks are locally controlled by their member banks. Once again, according to Black's Law Dictionary, we find that these privately owned banks actually issue money:

"Federal Reserve Act. Law which created Federal Reserve banks which act as agents in maintaining money reserves, issuing money in the form of bank notes, lending money to banks, and supervising banks. Administered by Federal Reserve Board (q.v.)".

The privately owned Federal Reserve (FED) banks actually issue (create) the "money" we use. In 1964, the House Committee on Banking and Currency, Subcommittee on Domestic Finance, at the second session of the 88th Congress, put out a study entitled *Money Facts* which contains a good description of what the FED is: *"The Federal Reserve is a total money-making machine. It can issue money or checks. And it never has a problem of making its checks good because it can obtain the $5 and $10 bills necessary to cover its check simply by asking the Treasury Department's Bureau of Engraving to print them"*.

Any one person or any closely knit group who has a lot of money has a lot of power. Now imagine a group of people who have the power to create money.

Imagine the power these people would have. This is exactly what the privately owned FED is!

No man did more to expose the power of the FED than Louis T. McFadden, who was the Chairman of the House Banking Committee back in the 1930's. In describing the FED, he remarked in the Congressional Record, House pages 1295 and 1296 on June 10, 1932:

"Mr. Chairman, we have in this country one of the most corrupt institutions the world has ever known. I refer to the Federal Reserve Board and the Federal reserve banks. The Federal Reserve Board, a Government Board, has cheated the Government of the United States and he people of the United States out of enough money to pay the national debt. The depredations and the iniquities of the Federal Reserve Board and the Federal reserve banks acting together have cost this country enough money to pay the national debt several times over. This evil institution has impoverished and ruined the people of the United States; has bankrupted itself, and has practically bankrupted our Government. It has done this through the maladministration of that law by which the Federal Reserve Board, and through the corrupt practices of the moneyed vultures who control it."

The FED is a central bank. Central banks are supposed to implement a country's fiscal policies. They monitor commercial banks to ensure that they maintain sufficient assets, like cash, so as to remain solvent and stable. Central banks also do business, such as currency exchanges and gold transactions, with other central banks. In theory, a central bank should be good for a country, and they might be if it wasn't for the fact that they are not owned or controlled by the government of the country they are serving. Private central banks, including our FED, operate not in the interest of the public good but for profit.

There have been three central banks in our nation's history. The first two, while deceptive and fraudulent, pale in comparison to the scope and size of the fraud being perpetrated by our current FED. What they all have in common is an insidious practice known as *"fractional banking."*

Fractional banking or fractional lending is the ability to create money from nothing, lend it to the government or someone else and charge interest to boot. The practice evolved before banks existed. Goldsmiths rented out space in their vaults to individuals and merchants for storage of their gold or silver. The goldsmiths gave these "depositors" a certificate that showed the amount of gold stored. These certificates were then used to conduct business.

In time the goldsmiths noticed that the gold in their vaults was rarely withdrawn. Small amounts would move in and out but the large majority never moved. Sensing a profit opportunity, the goldsmiths issued double receipts for the gold, in effect creating money (certificates) from nothing and then lending those certificates (creating debt) to depositors and charging them interest as well.

Since the certificates represented more gold than actually existed, the certificates were "fractionally" backed by gold. Eventually some of these vault operations were transformed into banks and the practice of fractional banking continued.

Keep that fractional banking concept in mind as we examine our first central bank, the First Bank of the United States (BUS). It was created, after bitter dissent in the Congress, in 1791 and chartered for 20 years. A scam not unlike the current FED, the BUS used its control of the currency to defraud the public and establish a legal form of usury.

This bank practiced fractional lending at a 10:1 rate, ten dollars of loans for each dollar they had on deposit. This misuse and abuse of their public charter continued for the entire 20 years of their existence. Public outrage over these abuses was such that the charter was not renewed and the bank ceased to exist in 1811.

The war of 1812 left the country in economic chaos, seen by bankers as another opportunity for easy profits. They influenced Congress to charter the second central bank, the Second Bank of the United States (SBUS), in 1816.

The SBUS was more expansive than the BUS. The SBUS sold franchises and literally doubled the number of banks in a short period of time. The country began to boom and move westward, which required money.

Using fractional lending at the 10:1 rate, the central bank and their franchisees created the debt/money for the expansion.

Things boomed for a while, then the banks decided to shut off the debt/money, citing the need to control inflation. This action on the part of the SBUS caused bankruptcies and foreclosures. The banks then took control of the assets that were used as security against the loans.

Closely examine how the SBUS engineered this cycle of prosperity and depression. The central bank caused inflation by creating debt/money for loans and credit and making these funds readily available. The economy boomed. Then they used the inflation which they created as an excuse to shut off the loans/credit/money.

The resulting shortage of cash caused the economy to falter or slow dramatically and large numbers of business and personal bankruptcies resulted. The central bank then seized the assets used as security for the loans. The wealth created by the borrowers during the boom was then transferred to the central bank during the bust. And you always wondered how the big guys ended up with all the marbles.

Now, who do you think is responsible for all of the ups and downs in our economy over the last 85 years? Think about the depression of the late '20s and all through the '30s The FED could have pumped lots of debt/money into the market to stimulate the economy and get the country back on track, but did they? No; in fact, they restricted the money supply quite severely. We all know the results that occurred from that action, don't we?

Why would the FED do this? During that period asset values and stocks were at rock bottom prices. Who do you think was buying everything at 10 cents on the dollar? I believe that it is referred to as consolidating the wealth. How many times have they already done this in the last 85 years? Do you think they will do it again?

Just as an aside at this point, look at today's economy. Markets are declining. Why? Because the FED has been very liberal with its debt/credit/money. The market was hyper inflated. Who creates inflation?

The FED. How does the FED deal with inflation? They restrict the debt/credit/money. What happens when they do that? The market collapses.

Alan Greenspan has said publicly on several occasions that he thinks the market is overvalued, or words to that effect. Just a hint that he will raise interest rates (restrict the money supply), and equity markets have a negative reaction. Governments and politicians do not rule central banks, central banks rule governments and politicians. President Andrew Jackson won the presidency in 1828 with the promise to end the national debt and eliminate the SBUS. During his second term President Jackson withdrew all government funds from the bank and on January 8, 1835, paid off the national debt. He is the only president in history to have this distinction. The charter of the SBUS expired in 1836.

Without a central bank to manipulate the supply of money, the United States experienced unprecedented growth for 60 or 70 years, and the resulting wealth was too much for bankers to endure. They had to get back into the game. So, in 1910 Senator Nelson Aldrich, then Chairman of the National Monetary Commission, in collusion with representatives of the European central banks, devised a plan to pressure and deceive Congress into enacting legislation that would covertly establish a private central bank.

This bank would assume control over the American economy by controlling the issuance of its money. After a huge public relations campaign, engineered by the foreign central banks, the Federal Reserve Act of 1913 was slipped through Congress during the Christmas recess, with many members of the Congress absent. President Woodrow Wilson, pressured by his political and financial backers, signed it on December 23, 1913.

The act created the Federal Reserve System, a name carefully selected and designed to deceive. *"Federal"* would lead one to believe that this is a government organization. *"Reserve"* would lead one to believe that the currency is being backed by gold and silver. *"System"* was used in lieu of the word "bank" so that one would not conclude that a new central bank had been created.

In reality, the act created a private, for profit, central banking corporation owned by a cartel of private banks. Who owns the FED? The Rothschilds of London and Berlin; Lazard Brothers of Paris; Israel Moses Seif of Italy;

Kuhn, Loeb and Warburg of Germany; and the Lehman Brothers, Goldman, Sachs and the Rockefeller families of New York.

Did you know that the FED is the only for-profit corporation in America that is exempt from both federal and state taxes? The FED takes in about one trillion dollars per year tax free! The banking families listed above get all that money.

Almost everyone thinks that the money they pay in taxes goes to the US Treasury to pay for the expenses of the government. Do you want to know where your tax dollars really go? If you look at the back of any check made payable to the IRS you will see that it has been endorsed as *"Pay Any F.R.B. Branch or Gen. Depository for Credit U.S. Treas. This is in Payment of U.S. Oblig."* Yes, that's right, every dime you pay in income taxes is given to those private banking families, commonly known as the FED, tax free.

Like many of you, I had some difficulty with the concept of creating money from nothing. You may have heard the term "monetizing the debt," which is kind of the same thing. As an example, if the US Government wants to borrow $1 million they go to the FED to borrow the money. The FED calls the Treasury and says print 10,000 Federal Reserve Notes (FRN) in units of one hundred dollars.

The Treasury charges the FED 2.3 cents for each note, for a total of $230 for the 10,000 FRNs. The FED then lends the $1 million to the government at face value plus interest. To add insult to injury, the government has to create a bond for $1 million as security for the loan. And the rich get richer. The above was just an example, because in reality the FED does not even print the money; it's just a computer entry in their accounting system. To put this on a more personal level, let's use another example.

Today's banks are members of the Federal Reserve Banking System. This membership makes it legal for them to create money from nothing and lend it to you. Today's banks, like the goldsmiths of old, realize that only a small fraction of the money deposited in their banks is ever actually withdrawn in the form of cash. Only about 4 percent of all the money that exists is in the form of currency. The rest of it is simply a computer entry.

Let's say you're approved to borrow $10,000 to do some home improvements. You know that the bank didn't actually take $10,000 from its pile of cash and put it into your pile? They simply went to their computer and input an entry of $10,000 into your account. They created, from thin air, a debt which you have to secure with an asset and repay with interest. The bank is allowed to create and lend as much debt as they want as long as they do not exceed the 10:1 ratio imposed by the FED.

It sort of puts a new slant on how you view your friendly bank, doesn't it? How about those loan committees that scrutinize you with a microscope before approving the loan they created from thin air. What a hoot! They make it complex for a reason. They don't want you to understand what they are doing. People fear what they do not understand. You are easier to delude and control when you are ignorant and afraid.

Now to put the frosting on this cake. When was the income tax created? If you guessed 1913, the same year that the FED was created, you get a gold star. Coincidence? What are the odds? If you are going to use the FED to create debt, who is going to repay that debt? The income tax was created to complete the illusion that real money had been lent and therefore real money had to be repaid. And you thought Houdini was good.

So, what can be done? My father taught me that you should always stand up for what is right, even if you have to stand up alone.

If *"We the People"* don't take some action now, there may come a time when "We the People" are no more. You should write a letter or send an email to each of your elected representatives. Many of our elected representatives do not understand the FED. Once informed they will not be able to plead ignorance and remain silent.

Article 1, Section 8 of the US Constitution specifically says that Congress is the only body that can *"coin money and regulate the value thereof."* The US Constitution has never been amended to allow anyone other than Congress to coin and regulate currency.

Ask your representative, in light of that information, how it is possible for the Federal Reserve Act of 1913, and the Federal Reserve Bank that it created, to be constitutional. Ask them why this private banking cartel is allowed to reap trillions of dollars in profits without paying taxes. Insist on an answer.

Thomas Jefferson said, *"If the America people ever allow private banks to control the issuance of their currencies, first by inflation and then by deflation, the banks and corporations that will grow up around them will deprive the people of all their prosperity until their children will wake up homeless on the continent their fathers conquered."*

Jefferson saw it coming 150 years ago. The question is, *"Can you now see what is in store for us if we allow the FED to continue controlling our country?"*

"The condition upon which God hath given liberty to man is eternal vigilance; which condition if he breaks, servitude is at once the consequence of his crime, and the punishment of his guilt."

INFORMATION FOR CLASSES
&
OTHER AUTHOR WORKS WE RECOMMEND

FREE ENTERPRISE FORUM
IBI Global, Inc.
200 Lime Quarry Road
Madison Alabama 35758
(256) 774-5444
www.ibiglobal.com

CHICKEN SOUP AND RELATED SEMINARS
Dr. Mark Victor Hansen & Associates
P.O. Box 7665
Newport Beach, CA 92658
(800) 433-2314
(714) 755-9304

ADVENTURES IN LEARNING
Dr. Lee Pulos
1260 Hornby St. /2nd Floor
Vancouver, BC V6Z 1W2
(604) 688-1714

ROBBINS RESEARCH
Anthony Robbins
9191 Town Center
Suite 600
San Diego, CA 92122
(619) 535-9900

SELF-ESTEEM SEMINARS
Jack Canfield
Chicken Soup and Self Esteem Seminars
Santa Barbara, CA
(800) 237-8336

PSI SEMINARS
Jane Willhite
Clearlake Oaks, CA
(707) 998-2222

LIFE SUCCESS ACADEMY PUBLISHING
200 Lime Quarry Road
Madison Alabama 35758
(256) 774-5444

DONATIONS FOR SUPER TEACHING FOR SCHOOLS
International Learning Trust
Corporate & Private Donations welcome
200 Lime Quarry Rd.
Madison, AL 35758
www.superteaching.org

Author Contact: BJ@IBIGlobal.com
LSA Publishing
200 Lime Quarry Road
Madison Alabama 35758